The Princely Press

Machiavelli on American Journalism

John Calhoun Merrill

University Press of America,® Inc.
Lanham • New York • Oxford

Copyright © 1998
University Press of America,® Inc.
4720 Boston Way
Lanham, Maryland 20706

12 Hid's Copse Rd.
Cummor Hill, Oxford OX2 9JJ

Library of Congress Cataloging-in-Publication Data

Merrill, John Calhoun
The princely press : Machiavelli on American journalism / John
Calhoun Merrill
p. cm.
Includes bibliographical references and index.
1. Journalistic ethics—United States. 2. Press and politics—United
States. 3. Freedom of the press—United States. 4. Machiavelli,
Niccolò, 1469-1527—Influence. I. Title.
PN4888.E8M43 1998 174'.9097 —DC21 98-10555 CIP

ISBN 0-7618-1035-8 (cloth: alk. ppr.)
ISBN 0-7618-1036-6 (pbk: alk. ppr.)

⊖™ The paper used in this publication meets the minimum
requirements of American National Standard for information
Sciences—Permanence of Paper for Printed Library Materials,
ANSI Z39.48—1984

A Modern Machiavellian Speaks:

"Do journalists sometimes write fiction and pass it off as fact? Do they use stolen material? Tape phone conversations without telling the person on the other end to beware? Misrepresent themselves in order to pry information from reluctant sources? . . . does this mean that journalists are unethical? As one who has done all of the above at one time or another, seldom with a feeling of shame and sometimes with a feeling of satisfaction for the results, I am inclined to pass over the ethical question entirely. If it works, I am generally for it.

"So long as reporters, vastly outnumbered and outgunned, are expected to penetrate these hostile areas [government and corporations] to obtain useful information, they can, I think, be forgiven for using almost any device or tactic so long as it enables them to bring back the bacon."

Robert Sherrill,
American Journalist

[From: "News Ethics: Press & Jerks," *Grand Street* 5, No. 2 (Winter 1986), 117.]

Contents

Foreword   ix

Machiavelli's Preface   xiii

Chapter 1:   Prelude to Interviews   1

Chapter 2:   A Preliminary Conversation   9

Chapter 3:   Journalists   17
appraisal; journalists and "mass man"; players with words; image; leadership; virtù and fortuna; the ideal journalist.

Chapter 4:   Mission   25
importance of success; creating an image; primacy of social control; tragedy of powerlessness; need for leadership and strong will; egocentrism; self-enhancement; manipulation; fooling the people; wielding power and changing society.

Chapter 5:   Power   35
key to political philosophy; journalistic dedication to power; getting and keeping power; press and government; successful use of power; achieving desired ends; press's pride in power; reasoned pragmatism; press monopoly on information; journalism and the law; using power.

Chapter 6:   Freedom   41
relativity of concept; connection between freedom and power; need to make better use of freedom; freedom--good and bad; comments on Thrasymachus, Socrates, and Plato;

freedom--key to power; freedom for all is anarchy; the fickle public; freedom and truth; antics with semantics.

Chapter 7:   Responsibility   51
definitions of responsibility; responsibility as obligation to succeed; norms of responsible journalism; use of people as a responsibility; low public taste; danger of altruistic action; responsibility begins at home; four uses of journalistic responsibility; egocentric pragmatics vs. social responsibility; conventional morality as danger to the press.

Chapter 8:   Self-Aggrandizement   59
importance of self-promotion; enlightened self-interest; Social Darwinism and the journalist; maximum autonomy; self-aggrandizement, basic journalistic assumptions; concern for self; motivation by anticipated success.

Chapter 9:   The State   65
relationship of press to state; constant struggle and ultimate state dominance; friction as socially useful; "using" one another; reason for state's fear of press; tendency to be timid; danger in playing by the rules; state's use of secrecy; comments on Thomas Jefferson.

Chapter 10:   The People   73
possession of little power; programmed to be led; people's voice no more than a "whine"; need for entertainment and hope-lifting; vagueness of public opinion; people have few expectations; people cannot be trusted; "best" and "worst" among people; selfishness in people; communitarian (public/civic) journalism; growth of public conformity; people's access to the press.

Chapter 11:   Objectivity   87
the myth of objectivity; subjectivity at base of all journalism; journalists a reality-strainers; basic desire to "grind axes"; the cloak of objectivity; reporting and personal biases; historians and journalists; problem of credibility; Press arrogance; a Press-created world.

Chapter 12:   Propaganda   **95**

*importance of rhetoric and propaganda to the Press;
conveying and originating propaganda; the purpose;
connotations of the term; people-manipulation; tailor-made
propaganda; appeal to emotions; assumed Press dedication
to the truth; game-playing with the truth; helplessness of the
public; types and prominence of press propaganda; natural
inclination to propagandize; good and bad
propaganda;need for persistance and craftiness; impact of
propaganda.*

Chapter 13:   Ends and Means   **103**

*Kant's error on ends and means; journalist seeing self as
"exception"; end as stimulus to action; justifying the means;
desire to succeed as motivation; need to lie and distort;
justification of means for success; use of illegal means in
reporting; tendency to compromise; concept of virtù; need to
use language loosely to reach goal and accomplish purpose.*

Chapter 14:   Ethics   **111**

*ethical consequentialism; pragmatism in lieu of ethics;
public and private ethics; egoism enthroned; altruism "if it
works"; too much worrying about ethics; ethics leads to
indecision and timidity; importance of reputation; adapting
when necessary; mystery of right and wrong; better to
exploit than to be exploited; problem with the "Golden
Rule."*

Chapter 15:   Postscript to the Interviews   **121**

Appendices   **127**

Select Bibliography   **133**

Index   **135**

About the Author   **139**

Foreword

Let there be no misunderstanding by the reader as to where the author-interviewer stands in respect to Machiavellian practices in journalism.

I am strongly opposed. In fact, my basic ethical stance is borrowed largely from Immanuel Kant who put, as I do today, great stock in basic Judeo-Christrian principles. and in the formulation of *a priori* principles or maxims to guide one in ethical decision-making. For Kant, unlike Machiavelli, consequences were unimportant; duty to principle was the important thing. Probably the best antidote for Machiavellianism is a good dose of Kantian moral philosophy.

During my almost half-century of teaching at the university level, I have consistently tried to instill in students a *non-Machiavellian* perspective in ethics. This has not been easy at times because the temptations to succeed and to win prizes are very strong and the pragmatic position espoused by Machiavelli is appealing. Also, as I think the interviews in this little book will show, Machiavelli was a complex person and much that he said seems to make a great deal of sense.

Machiavelli personifies the cunning and crafty person who (at least in his or her *public or institutional* life) would lead others away from traditional ethical paths into the highways of pragmatics where success is king. And quite often he does this with grace and charm and the demeanor of one who is moderate, reasonable, and well-spoken.

It is my hope that the exposure to Machiavelli on the following pages will cause journalists to react against the dark side of journalism and to see more than success as a challenging and worthy ambition, even if some failures ensue and some prizes are lost. It is also my hope that this little book might also serve to indicate to the lay (non-journalist) reader the terrific pragmatic temptations facing the journalist every day.

Regardless of the unusual concept and interview format, this is a book with scholarly foundations. Its content stems from the author's reading of Machiavelli's works and many of the scholarly works *about* Machiavelli. And further, this book represents a serious attempt to adapt a general political philosophy to the field of modern journalism. If Machiavelli *could* write about American journalism today, I have no doubt but that his ideas would be much the same as I have him expressing in this series of interviews that follow.

Many critics in recent years have described American journalism as "Machiavellian," or as having basic tendencies in that direction. I believe that, overall, this is unfair as a blanket indictment, although such tendencies do manifest themselves far too often. There are Machiavellian journalists (such as Robert Sherrill quoted in the frontispiece, and others more moderate) among us, but such voices surely represent but a small segment of American journalism. But when one considers the big publishers, media managers, and other journalistic leaders in the country {whose views and tactics are largely unknown as they grab for growth and the big bucks} it may well be that American journalism is more Machiavellian than we suspect.

At any rate, Machiavellian journalism is consistent with the traditional hard-nosed, success-oriented American journalism. However much the journalist tries to repel it, it stands at the door and knocks. Why, some readers might ask, should Machiavelli be given a chance to express his opinions about journalism? Might not this be counter-productive by giving too much attention to his philosophy and thereby causing more cynicism in the public and painting a negative and gloomy picture that might well discourage the idealistic present and future journalist? It certainly *should not*, this book simply presents the paradigmatic "Machiavellian" position on the press. It does not subscribe to such a position, and certainly it does not *recommend* it.

I feel such a book is valuable to all people who are interested in the American press. In a real sense, we are all "press people" since we get our view of the world through journalism. Journalists and journalism students especially should find Machiavelli's perspectives interesting since they are enmeshed deeply in this tempting world of success and competition. This book describes an aspect of contemporary journalism that cannot be ignored: a strain that can be called egocentric, pragmatic, power-hungry, ends-oriented journalism. It also introduces to the context of journalism a fascinating figure of the early Italian Renaissance and one of history's most controversial thinkers: Niccolò Machiavelli.

Journalists and prospective journalists need to look at the dark side of their craft. They need to examine their own motives and their own tactics. Such a book as this, I believe, will (in an unorthodox way, admittedly) focus attention on *journalistic ethics*. At any rate, it should aid in raising ethical consciousness and helping journalists wrestle with their attempt to decide whether to act morally (using traditional or private ethics) or to act pragmatically (using special or public ethics).

The *pragmatic* pull is great, especially for strong-willed and conscientious journalists, and Machiavelli speaks loudly for this position. It is hoped that, by dealing with this "success-orientation" in journalism, this book may by indirection help push journalists in another direction: toward a concern for personal authenticity, honesty, self-respect, virtue, and public trust.

John C. Merrill
University of Missouri
1998

Machiavelli's Preface

John Merrill was good enough to let me have a look at the manuscript of this book after he had a first draft done. And, at his request, I am happy to write this brief preface. I was, for the most part, satisfied with the draft, although perhaps he tended to cast me as a rather callous and simplistic person of amoral or immoral inclinations. This is, of course, quite natural, for it is the *vulgar* Machiavelli that history has mainly made me out to be. Merrill, understandably for his purposes, has chosen to reiterate this dominant or dark dimension of my beliefs as they relate to his area of special interest--journalism. But I must admit that he was much kinder to me than I had expected.

It is quite true that historians, politicians, and philosophers have generally treated me as a diabolical, evil person, an image stressed by the American, Leo Strauss, but some scholars in Merrill's own day have tended to interpret me in a more favorable way, even placing me in the mainstream of civic humanism. I think that is a bit excessive, and Merrill's view that conforms with general historical opinion of me as a dissembler is rather closer to the truth.

Although I must admit the validity of most of the ideas Merrill chose to take from the interviews, and the accuracy of most of the quotations he solicited from me, I do feel that a few of my views have been somewhat misrepresented. These are not really important, however, and the non-specialized reader can get a generally valid idea of my thought regarding journalism. Any misleading information in this book is not, I think, because of intentional bias on Merrill's part; rather it is a result of the brevity of the interviews and the author's hazy understanding of the intellectual Florentine culture of my day. But, discounting the natural impediments of time and culture, I have no serious objections to the general tenor of the book. I would suggest to the reader, however, that if he wishes to have a more detailed and comprehensive view of my thought that he read at least *The Prince*, and perhaps *The Discourses*. And there are, of course, many commentaries on my work and some rather good biographies.

I must say that Merrill was a considerate and thorough interviewer and, unlike most Florentines I am familiar with, he was always on time for the sessions. Many of my quotes recorded in the book are somewhat truncated, perhaps due to our rather short sessions and the haste with which he had to take notes. It was obvious to me that the author disagreed with most of my ideas about journalism, but he listened patiently and, by and large, gave me a good hearing. At one point I asked him if he did not want to argue with me in the book. He said that he did not, that he mainly wanted his readers to get my views on a number of aspects of journalism. They could, if they desired, have their own arguments with me.

I would hasten to insist that I always have been honest and forthright in the expression of my opinions, except of course, when it is not expedient for me to do so. But I assure the reader that I was completely candid and sincere during the series of interviews with the author. Although, as I said earlier, some scholars are busy giving me a more positive image, I have written, and sincerely believe, that human beings never do anything good except by necessity and that excessive freedom leads to disorder. This is why, as I say in the following interviews, the typical audiences of journalism need firm guidance, and freedom is not necessarily good for them.

Journalists should understand this concept in respect to their audiences. They should realize that, in general, people are desirous of leadership, searching for saviors, and are easily led and easily corrupted. Certainly, as I have written, they are pretenders and dissemblers, ungrateful, fickle, evaders of danger, and out after easy gain. Certain scholars in Merrill's day may well write that I really don't mean such things, but I assure you that I do.

And so, dear reader, as you begin to follow my ideas on the following pages, please know that I and my thoughts have been interpreted in many ways by such intellects as Benedetto Croce, Isaiah Berlin, Friedrich Meineche, Leo Strauss, and Anthony Parel. Ultimately, of course, only *I* know what I mean by my words. But I have tried to relate the meaning of some of them, at least in the area of journalism, to John Merrill. He, like Berlin, Strauss, and dozens of others who have concentrated their thinking on me, will have to dip his own net into my words, pulling from them his own meaning.

Some of my statements will undoubtedly be misinterpreted, especially those that appear extreme, and even mean-spirited in nature. For example, I have emphasized the need to push, push, to give no quarter to a foe. But one should remember one of my favorite sayings: *Non fu mai partito savio condursa el nemico alla disperazione.* Roughly in English it means that it has never been a good policy to drive an enemy to desperation. So even in my more dramatic moments I plead *non culpabilis* to dysfunctional extremism.

And as has happened so many times, the author's interpretations of my ideas will be challenged and disputed. And those who challenge will have *their* interpretations challenged. And on and on. In conclusion, all I can say here is that Merrill, in spite of many problems, one of which is that he comes to my ideas from the field of journalism, has done a quite satisfactory job. The words of mine which he has recorded will probably not please many readers, especially those who have been dipped deeply in the Judeo-Christian moral tradition. But I'll have to live (or better, die) with that.

Niccolò Machiavelli
(San Casciano, 1522)

Chapter 1

Prelude to Interviews

This book draws almost exclusively on Niccolò Machiavelli (1469-1527), whose *The Prince* set the political stage for the expedient, pragmatic, and successful practitioner in social relations. For many years I have observed with increasing fascination activities in journalism which I have identified with Machiavelli. At long last I have summoned the nerve to venture somewhat into the realm of historical imagination by trying to relate Machiavelli's advice for rulers of the late 15th and early 16th century Italian city-states to journalism in America as the 21st century dawns.

In order to do this I have devised a series of interviews with Machiavelli at his home just outside Florence. Actually, what I am doing is propelling myself back in time to the year 1520, seven years before the famed political philosopher and historian died. In conducting these interviews, I am indulging my penchant for imaginative adventure as well as my interest in intellectual history commingled as it is with the joy of philosophical musing.

Machiavelli, as is well known, was a devotee of power--or at least an advocate of power for those who would rule successfully. And modern journalism, especially as conducted in the world's economically and politically advanced nations today, has become a powerful social instrument. Whether in the United States or in China, it is considered an instrumental adjunct.to cultural development and a necessary social agenda-setter. And even in the so-called"developing nations" (the Third World), like Nigeria or Bangladesh, journalism propels the Ship of State through hazardous waters and surrounds the captain with considerable power (however briefly). What would Machiavelli say about this journalism? The prospect of an answer propelled me into this project.

Few would deny that journalism, although sometimes rather impotent, means power. And it follows that press people, especially those who are in control, wield considerable influence in society. Journalism's power is used in different ways in different societies, but the common factor everywhere is contained in this basic journalistic question: **How can we achieve our ends?** I had a feeling that Machiavelli just might enjoy ruminating on this question.

As I see it, a business-like, lean, impersonal, bottom-line-oriented, corporate journalism has developed since the early 19th century in America. It is increasingly the journalism of chains, groups, and ever-expanding media networks--resulting in a journalism where decisions are made in board rooms by businessmen and lawyers instead of in newsrooms by editors. In the last years of the 20th century another trend or orientation was making inroads on media editorial autonomy--**communitarianism**, with its media genre of "public" or "civic" journalism. Basically this new trend was attempting to inject the public into editorial decision-making and to shift journalism's stance from one of neutrality and non-involvement to one of advocacy and involvement. In an era of increasing public criticism of media, putting on a new face as "public" or "civic" journalism is only a new way of trying to succeed. New means to a success-oriented end is only natural.

Nothing new here. The American journalistic tradition has always been practical, success-driven, competitive, and power-hungry. Today it has become simply more expansive, more efficient in its business operations, and seemingly more concerned with "democratizing" than ever before. In many ways Thomas Hobbes' governmental *Leviathan* has, in the modern world, become the Press.

But along with this basic American journalism of pragmatism, power, and profit, has been a more idealistic strain. The intellectual giants of Enlightenment Europe and early America (18th and 19th centuries) muted the earlier pragmatism of the Renaissance and had a significant impact on the development of American journalism--one dedicated to profit and power as well as to public service. Such men as John Locke, Voltaire, John Stuart Mill, Jefferson and Madison contributed to it a social conscience, a sense of responsibility and a moral foundation that is--to some degree--still with us.

Not really so, say the communitarians. For them the Enlightenment liberal ideas may have been all right for that time, but not for today. Press excesses have been spawned by Enlightenment liberal ideas, which, according to the communitarians, must be purged from journalism..

It is true that hiding within the Enlightenment-inspired journalism was a pragmatic core which is basically egoistic and success-oriented. It supplied American journalism with one question (How can I succeed and gain power?) to supplement the other question (How can I help others and help society progress?). The first question, I contend, was introduced to American journalism by Machiavelli, Hobbes, Adam Smith, and other thinkers.

So, granting there has been a strong strain of idealistic, altruistic "public concern" journalism in American history, we must admit that along with such positive journalism has been a deep current of exploitive journalism: that which has mainly benefited the journalists, not the public. This current has included strong portions of journalistic self-interest, lowest-common-denominator communication, sensationalism and poor taste. Many critics of American journalism, like the members of the Hutchins Commission of the 1940s, have noted such practices and have called them "irresponsible."

American journalists, in seeking their objectives and in achieving their ends, often evidence Machiavellian tendencies. Although normally we associate Machiavelli with *evil or unethical end*s, such an image may be somewhat unfair. Even the most socially conscious, altruistic editor may use Machiavellian tactics from time to time. It is the firmness and determination, the skill and cunning, the virtuosity by which a journalist seeks success that determines his or her status as a Machiavellian. In defining Machiavellianism one must look *at the means employed* and not at the ends desired.

In the interviews that follow we shall see that "Old Nick," as Machiavelli is often less-than-affectionately called, is not decisively bad; rather he, like many journalists today, is only "bad" when he needs to be, when socially accepted tactics fail in the achievement of his goals. Old Nick, a name Niccolò Machiavelli has shared with the devil, is indeed a crafty person who has given us what is probably the first and basic blueprint for successful, though often unethical, journalism.

Machiavelli had much to say, especially in *The Prince* (completed in 1514) and *Discourses* (1519), about tactics of power and success which have been used to great advantage by American journalists. Walter Lippmann has said that Machiavelli is one of the most reviled men in history, but that he probably has the greatest number of followers.

The reader of the following interviews may well conclude that American journalism is primarily *Machiavellian*--meaning that it is power-based, competitive, ends-oriented, egocentric, and pragmatic. Others may dispute this. A case can be made, I'm sure, for American journalism as an enterprise of integrity, selflessness and public betterment. But Machiavellian values do not comport with such altruistic practice and readers can come to their own conclusions about the basic nature of American journalism.

The intent of this book is to let Machiavelli himself talk about American journalism. This will be done through the brief introductory conversation with him, followed by a series of twelve interviews with him (conducted by the author) in 1520 at Machiavelli's small estate at San Casciano just outside Florence.

Who was Machiavelli? Let us set the stage: He was an Italian political philosopher, historian, poet, and playwright born in Florence in 1469. He was first to develop the idea that political leaders are not bound by conventional morality and to insist that power and its cunning use is of utmost importance. His life was divided between an active political period and a time of retirement when he did most of his writing. All of his important books were written after 1512 when he was relieved of his governmental functions in Florence.

Machiavelli was a good reporter, although he did not work for any journal. He was a keen observer. He travelled widely, observing political conditions in Europe--especially in France and Germany--during the first decade of the 16th century. His reports have been preserved and show a keen understanding of political institutions and politics.

Like many modern journalists, Machiavelli was a political person and historian. He was also an ethicist of sorts, dealing in his works with "public morality" (success-oriented) instead of "private morality" (virtue-oriented). He was the first political (read: journalistic) thinker to develop the idea that morality differs from and is not bound by the usual ethical norms. He also introduced the important concept that power is the decisive factor in political (read: journalistic) life.

Machiavelli was a firm believer in success, in power, in pragmatics. In many ways, he was in his day much like many American editors and publishers. He was goal-oriented; he believed in advising and directing the government; he was somewhat abrasive, even arrogant; he was an agenda-setter; he was a pragmatist; he was aware of his expertise in almost every area; he believed the prince (leader) was above and beyond accountability; he had an answer to almost every question; he believed in having objectives and pursuing them vigorously and by any means; he believed in taking definite stands but modifying them if necessary to achieve goals, and he believed in order and organization.

In ethics, if he can be thought of as ethical at all, he had an overriding Kantian maxim (about the only thing Kantian about him) which seemed to combine both duty and consequences; it might be expressed like this: *Do those things which will maximize personal success.* He would bind today's journalists to such a deontological principle, one that is obviously an egoistic one. This is not the course for the altruistic journalist, but nobody has contended that Machiavelli was an altruist.

By all means succeed, Machiavelli would tell today's journalist. And also, by *any* means. Achieve your objective, he would say. Get that story. Of course, if getting the story goes against your goal or "end," then do not get it. Or, it is possible that Machiavelli would advise the journalist to get only those parts of the story consistent with the overall purpose. So actually he would see journalistic tactics as effective or ineffective, not as ethical or unethical. Many scholars contend that Machiavelli appeared more wicked than he really was, that he desired to shock his contemporaries and therefore wrote blunt maxims that gave him a reputation for immorality. It has been said that really he was a good citizen, a church-goer, a good father of five children, and a generally upright man. Be this as it may, this book of interviews deals with his preachments and advance, not with the reality of his character. Scholars will continue to study and debate this.

Most of the philosophy used in the following interviews with Machiavelli is based on chapters from *The Prince*; it was a guide to power politics, presenting Cesare Borgia as the ideal prince, and providing the politician (and the journalist) with a success-oriented recipe for success. Especially chapters 15 through 25 of *The Prince* deal with the basic principles of conduct which should be used by the succcessful ruler. Machiavelli's preachments became a target of attacks by the Catholic Counter-Reformation, and the French, who hated the Italians, coined "Machiavellianism," as a term of opprobrium. Other basic Machiavellian concepts adapted for use in this book come from *Discourses*, a more detailed and deliberate book than *The Prince*, completed in 1519--a year prior to the prescient interviews appearing on the following pages. I call them "prescient" interviews because, at least in my opinion, they evince Machiavelli's foreknowledge of journalism's future in modern America.

In spite of my eagerness to interview Machiavelli, I must admit that, even in these imaginary sessions, I approached the man with considerable trepidation. His image of cold intellect and craftiness was well known. But since I had early found myself contemplating the parallels I noted between his ideas (especially those in *The Prince*) and many of the basic concepts of modern American journalism, I was determined to let him speak on the subject. After considerable correspondence with Machiavelli (in English since I do not know Italian, French, or Latin), I arranged to be in Florence during the month of August, 1520. He agreed to meet me for a short introductory conversation, and then to grant me twelve interviews (short ones, he insisted) on topics of my choosing.

The year 1520 was a busy year for Machiavelli. He was at his home in San Casciano, about seven miles outside Florence, where he was working hard to finish two books--*Arte della Guerra* and *La Vita di Castruccio Gastracani da Lucca.* It was here at his modest dwelling that the interviews were held. Contrary to his reputation, Machiavelli was quite friendly--even cordial--and somewhat shy. In spite of his failing health (he was to die seven years later), he was lively in general demeanor and style of expression.

Machiavelli's rhetorical mannerisms have been described in depth by many scholars and should be mentioned here. His style was generally terse and direct, although at times he seemed to express his views with deliberate vagueness or ambiguity. He did not define his terms very well, assuming that he and I fully understood one another. He was impatient with my early attempts to get him to be more precise with definitions, and I found myself interrupting him less and less as the interviews proceeded. He enjoyed using terms, especially abstract ones, as if they had universal meaning. And, since I did not want to cause him pain, and because he insisted that the interviews be brief, I decided to live with the semantic problem.

Machiavelli, like all Italian writers of the period, tended to overstatement. He appeared somewhat moderate in his interviews with me, certainly more so than he had been in *The Prince*, but even so the reader will note a certain flamboyant quality in his rhetoric. Since he liked almost everything about the days of imperial Rome, Machiavelli scattered Latin words and phrases through the interview, referring often (straying from the journalistic thrust of certain questions) to certain Latin quotations from Livy, Tacitus, Virgil, and Justinus. This he had also done in his *Discourses*, which he had recently completed.

He delighted in sweeping statements, generalizations, bold shocking verbal jabs. He was an artist, but also an analyst; he was intuitive rather than logical, and he loved to dramatize his remarks and conclusions so as to achieve the greatest impact. He sat with his right leg crossed over the left one, upright in a heavy straight chair with a window always behind him. He was serious in his answers, never laughing and seldom smiling. He seemed genuinely interested in talking about journalism, and manifested a self-assurance that was remarkable when talking about journalistic matters of the future. Good historians (of which he was one), he insisted, should know a great deal about the future; this is one reason, he said, that one studies history.   Machiavelli, during the interviews, was self-assured; he was not pessimistic, but realistic; not cynical, but skeptical; not rude, but direct; not naive, but worldly-wise; not superficial, but impatient with verbosity. Certain key terms dominated his rhetoric, terms which tended to shed familiar light on his personal values--words like *ambition, will, luck, liberty, order, persuasion, ability, cunning,*and *courage.*

So the reader will get a feel for the appearance of this man, Machiavelli, let me describe him briefly. Whenever I entered his sitting room or what he called his "writing room" (a rather small bookladen alcove off the entrance hall), he greeted me cordially and showed me to a chair facing his. He did, at this point, smile almost imperceptibly. He was just under six feet tall, of slender build, with sparkling eyes. His head was small, with an aquiline nose and a tightly closed mouth which stretched into a straight line. He gave every sign of being a good listener, a keen observer, and a deep thinker.

Once an interview had begun, he came across as a rather cold person who was psychoanalyzing me as he watched me, listened to my questions, and answered in a rather slow, calculating way. There was a suggestion of sarcasm in his flashing eyes and in the twitching of his narrow lips. He had an air of confidence which showed itself in his bearing and in the force with which he gave his answers. He never seemed to stall or to grope for a word. It must be admitted that he was not the easiest person to interview. Even though he was answering questions, he had the knack of leading the interview, of bending it to his desires.

So here he was: Machiavelli being interviewed during the month of August, 1520, in his home just outside Florence. He agreed to a dozen sessions--plus a short introductory conversation in which he would set the ground-rules for the interviews. He was no journalist of course, he admitted, but he *could* be one. Nothing exceptional about being a journalist, he said. Any reasonable person with a good education and a sensitivity to other people and to the realities of social and political life could be a journalist. And, he said--with a faint smile flicking at the corners of his mouth--the basic principles of journalism would be the same in the year 2020 as they always have been. Principles, according to Old Nick (he permitted me to call him simply Nick), do not change. Only technology changes--and people, of course, although they to change very little through history. He admitted that technology going into the 21st century would probably change the nature of journalism, but would have little or nothing to do with the basic principles of journalistic reporting and rhetoric.

These interviews that follow focus on Machiavelli's ideas about journalism, about certain *principles* related to the mass media, and especially about the values, character, and techniques of those who participate in journalism's positions of leadership. Many (perhaps *most*) modern media people will, of course, disagree with Machiavelli; some will be incensed at his negative, pragmatic vision of American journalism which they will find unrealistic. Some will feel that the interviewer himself is the culprit--making Machiavelli say things that he really would not have said.

The author, or interviewer if you wish, pleads guilty to some distortion. Certain questions were *not* asked; others were given too much attention, perhaps. Everything that Machiavelli said could not be used, but this should not surprise modern journalists. But it should be stated that, like most modern journalists, I have *tried* faithfully to represent the ideas of Machiavelli as they bear on journalism today.

So now, without further ado, let us proceed with our interviews with Machiavelli at his home outside of Florence. The date is August 1, 1520. I arrive for my appointment at 10 o'clock in the morning in a drizzly haze that hangs over over the small estate.

Chapter 2

A Preliminary Conversation

[August 1, 1520]

JM: Good morning, sir. I am very happy to meet you and I hope that our talks about journalism will go well.

NM: They should, I think. That is if you will, through your questions, keep me on the subject. I'm prone to roam all over the intellectual landscape, you know. I understand from your last letter to me that today you wish only to meet me and to set some ground rules (as you put it) for the twelve sessions you requested.

JM: That's right, sir.

NM: You can forget that "sir" business. Just call me Machiavelli--or if you wish, you may call me "Nick." I actually like that name, although it is somewhat informal for us Florentines. I understand that many have referred to me as "Old Nick, which obviously has a negative connotation. But Nick itself is rather straightforward, and friendly enough.

JM: Great. I'll call you Nick, although perhaps that's a little familiar since, as you probably know, your fame has spread almost everywhere in the world.

NM: Yes, I know. In many ways the attention which has been, and is being, paid to me is quite surprising.

JM: I really do appreciate your taking time to have these interviews with me during this month. I know you are very busy--putting the final touches on your *Discourses,* writing two other books, and planning a history of Florence, just commissioned by the Pope.

NM: Yes, I am almost always busy. That's how one gets things done. But I do take some time off, roam about the fields catching a few birds, and talking with friends at the tavern across the way.

JM: Well, anyway, let's talk about the upcoming interviews for a few minutes. After this introductory session today, what I hope we can do is to have a dozen rather brief interviews on topics I wish to get your perspectives on. We can decide on specific dates of interviews as we go along. Is this all right?

NM: Fine. But I must insist that the sessions be short--no more than an hour, and that they are finished by the end of August. Next month I will be over in Florence, and I hope down in Rome having some talks with Pope Clement about the history of Florence he wishes me to undertake.

JM: No problem. We'll keep the sessions short, and will finish before the month is over. For a few minutes this morning I hope we can talk generally about journalism so as to provide a background for the more specific interviews to come. Would you say a few words about your qualifications to speak about journalism or to give advice to journalists?

NM: Well, let me say something about myself, something which might surprise you. In addition to being an enlightened and thoughtful person, I am really a very friendly, and even ethical, person, one who wants to right wrongs and create a better society based on the Roman Republic. But to your question. Actually I am a true journalist at heart; I am therefore *per se* qualified to discourse on anything. But beyond that, I know that journalism is power. Journalists need advice from someone like me to keep them connected with power.Too many journalists are soft and have muddled brains due to too much concern with conventional ethics.

JM: Do you know many journalists?

NM: Not really. And I am perhaps fortunate in that respect. As you know, there are actually no such persons around in my day, but their prototypes--the politicians--are everywhere trying to change the world to conform to their concepts. So-called journalists are coming before long, but they will not be significantly different from the political scribes and rhetoricians who inform and persuade the people on the street corners, the parks, and in the courts. Actually you might say that I personify the journalists of my day, being Florence's version of your Walter Lippmann or perhaps George Will..

JM: You wrote what is perhaps your most famous book, *Il Principe* (We call it *The Prince*) six years ago. I hear about it everywhere, but it has still to be published. Do you hope to have a publisher soon, and how does it relate to journalism?

NM: No publisher yet, but there are some possibilities down in Rome. It's a very good book and, of course, will be published. As you know, *adversis etenim frangi non esse virorum.* Or as you might say, you can't keep a good man down. Sorry I slip into Latin occasionally. What's so good about *The Prince* is that it is in accord with human nature. The world is full of people who want to succeed, to gain power, to direct others. My book, *The Prince,* as you call it, gives them the proper tactics to achieve their goal. It's based, you know, on my observation of the actual practices of my old acquaintance, Cesare Borgia. He was successful...not always liked, you know, but he was effective in building his principality, giving it stability, and providing a good life for its citizens. He was a man of action, and *virtus in actione consistit.* So I decided to share his concepts with my fellow Florentines and with posterity in *The Prince.* Now, what was the second part of the question?

JM: How does *The Prince* relate to journalism?

NM: Oh, yes. Well, what is good for the politician is good for *any* power-hungry person. And the journalist, because of his basic work, is power-hungry. In fact, most journalists are simply frustrated politicians anyway. I'm sure we'll discuss this later in one of the interview sessions. But here I can say that *The Prince* gives the recipe for personal success. The journalist will find it useful.

JM: But, Nick, many journalists don't agree with your ideas about succeeding by any means. They want to be ethical. If they succeed, good; if not, that's all right, too. Don't you think that's the proper way to do journalism?

NM: Maybe in 10,000 years. But not now, nor any time soon. People are just not ready for non-pragmatic morality. Success is the name of the game. If deceit is needed in journalism, it must be used. One must do what is necessary. One must fight trickery with trickery, not with good will and honesty. If you don't, you'll lose every time.

JM: I don't want to pursue this much further at this time, but we'll get back to it in one of the interviews. But it does seem to me that journalists of my day are interested in a kind of democratization of the newspaper, an outgrowth of a movement called *communitarianism*, and many are stressing the need to put the public welfare ahead of their own interests. Isn't that a good, responsible idea?

NM: No, no. You have the mistaken idea that democracy is good. It is bad for everybody -- at least in the real world we live in. People want authority. They want to be told. Your editors and news directors recognize that, for they are in the business of *telling,* of telling audiences what they should know, what they should think, and the like. A newspaper (or a State) should be run by an absolute despot. Civic freedom may be injured, of course, but most citizens don't really want it. Think of what your newspapers would look like if the people had a hand in determining the appearance, content, and policies. Chaos. No, democracy just won't do the job, in a state or in a newspaper. As I've said, maybe democracy's day will come in some pale, insipid, conformist, computer-driven world of the future, but it will be a long time coming.

JM: But it worked in Greece, didn't it?

NM: Not really. Do you call the system of sexism and slavery that existed in the time of Socrates democracy? I don't. And remember that Plato and other thinkers were certainly not sold on democracy. Have you read *The Republic*? I must say that a good dictator who is strong and intelligent is exactly what is needed in a newspaper or in a principality.

JM: But shouldn't the editor or publisher want to be highly thought of by his colleagues?

NM: No. Remember what I have written: To be feared gives more security than to be loved. Workers like a strong leader. Respect is better than love, and respect comes from power, not from sentimental gestures.

JM: But can a person be virtuous by being powerful?

NM: Virtue *is* strength. The *virtuoso* is never a weak person. Weakness makes a person timid and afraid to take chances, to make decisions. Of course, this person of *virtù* may make mistakes--in the sense of not accomplishing his objectives--but even these mistakes, if admitted, will lead to a strengthening resolve and character.

JM: How could a journalist have freedom in a system such as you propose?

NM: Many journalists cannot, of course. They are basically robots, functionaries, slaves. And that's all they want to be. But others, of stronger will, can attain some freedom, and with it power. But actually the publishers and editors have the freedom. And so they have the real power. The two go together. If I want freedom, I seek power. That is the secret. Unfortunately., or fortunately, most people don't understand that principle.

JM: That is all very interesting, your remarks about freedom being in the hands of the elite core of journalists. But I am interested in how this impinges on education, and on the education for journalists especially.

NM: Well, education certainly relates to this idea of the freedom-power relationship. Journalists, of course, are exposed to differing educational philosophies in your country. There are the skills-oriented programs, those that you call "professional" programs, and then there is the more theoretical, general, and liberal arts focus provided in other programs from which students find their way into journalism. It would seem . . .

JM: But how do these two approaches, which I think you are right in identifying, relate to journalists who are likely to have power and those who are not?

NM: I was just getting to that. It would seem to me that those students who are skills-oriented, who want to get what you call "hands-on" training, and who emphasize so-called professional courses are the ones who are generally destined to be functionaries, followers, cogs in the machine. They have no real desire to think and deal with ideas. They have no real desire for freedom and power, and are content to relinquish their potential power to others, to fit snugly into a rather passive niche, and to escape making many decisions and using what freedom they have. In so doing, they forfeit power.

JM: And those opting for another kind of education for journalism?

NM: Those intent on garnering a good general education, one stressing history, philosophy, and literature. These are the students who will most likely take leadership or power positions in journalism. The kind of education they seek is an indication of their future direction. Specific skills of the journalist, for these "non-professional" students, can be picked up very quickly on the job by any reasonably intelligent person, so there is no need to sacrifice substantive course-work for such "hands-on" courses.

JM: But what, then, are these general-education students interested in during their university years?

NM: In such courses as I mentioned a moment ago. Courses that will help them better understand other people and their social institutions. Courses that give them insights into the truly great minds of the past, and courses that give them a chance to develop innovative strategies for dealing with ideas and people. Courses should stimulate thinking, but most are little more than redundant activity. . .

JM: What do you mean by "redundant activity"?

NM: Well, it's simple. I mean courses that get students to do some operation, basically the same one, repeatedly. Simply filling time, and stressing rules and effort over the acquisition of knowledge and wisdom. To most good students this time-consuming, redundant learning activity is tedious and demeaning.

JM: But not all prospective journalists are naturally good writers or editors or advertising layout persons. They need repetitive practice to get them to a professional level where they can provide the basic services needed. Shouldn't they get this in the university?

NM: You are right of course. The vast majority of journalism aspirants are in need of basic skills. Of course, they *should* have developed many of them in their pre-university years, but as we both know, most of them don't. So perhaps you are right: perhaps journalism educators do need to provide some skills--but remember that, as they do so, they are directing this training, and I purposely call it *training* and not education, at those who are destined to be followers, functionaries in journalism and not at those who will have the power and freedom: the leaders in journalism.

JM: But isn't it difficult for a student specializing (we call it "majoring") in something like philosophy or Russian literature to be proficient in, let's say, writing?

NM: Not at all. For example, I received my early education, almost all of it, from a well-known Latin teacher, Paulo da Ronciglione. Of course, I did get some vital learning during my stint at the University of Florence. But mainly my formal education came from a teacher of Latin. I wrote, of course, for him, and he criticized my writing. And I had long and mentally stimulating conversations with him on a wide assortment of subjects. I didn't study rhetoric or linguistics *per se*, although I must admit I had ample opportunity to delve into those areas.

JM: But if you had specifically studied communication skills, wouldn't that have helped you?

NM: I doubt it. I got these skills along with my study of history, philosophy, and the politics of Rome and Athens. And certainly my deep study of Latin helped me in appreciating the thought and culture of Rome and its great thinkers, like Pliny and Virgil, that came out of that classical age. I also think that a study of Latin would help your journalist handle English more correctly and skillfully.

JM: But wouldn't you have been a better reporter and journal-keeper in your subsequent career as a diplomat or foreign emissary if you had studied interview techniques and the proper forms of courtly reportage?

NM: Not at all. As you probably know, I am considered a very good writer, a keen observer of the human condition, a perceptive critic, and a natural psychologist, political scientist, and historian. I doubt if I would even be as good as I am had I studied such "skills" courses as you mention.

JM: Well, Nick, I think we should stop now. I know you have many other things to do, and I must see to my lodgings over in Florence. I'll see you again the day after tomorrow, as you suggested, to talk more specifically about journalists themselves, who they are, and who they ought to be. Thank you very much for seeing me this morning and for this interesting initial conversation. Farewell.

Chapter 3

Journalists

[August 3, 1520]

JM: Well, Nick, in this first interview I would like to have you talk about *journalists themselves*, about the types of persons who are journalists, about their quality, their characteristics, et cetera. I realize that this is a rather general topic and that you will likely stray into other related areas, but let's try to concentrate on the *persona* of what you think is the typical journalist.

NM: No problem. All topics are essentially general; I can handle this one... and, as to my straying, some of my best observations are in oblique references.

JM: Well, how do you see my contemporaries as journalists? Just give some of your insights and I'll try to follow them up with more specific questions.

NM: First, I must say that too many journalists are shallow thinkers. Perhaps they feel that thinking is not really important, that what they need to be are simply recording machines, transmission robots, going off in all directions as they present a world far worse than the shadows on Plato's cave wall. Chaotic and shallow thinkers--that is what I would call most of your journalists. Their minds are not disciplined; therefore how can their journalism be well-ordered and meaningful? I would say that...

JM: Forgive me, Nick, but I must follow up on that. It seems to me that you are thinking of journalists as *reporters*. But you must know that we have many other kinds of journalists--feature writers, essayists, editorial writers, and the like. Are you calling all of them shallow thinkers?

NM: Of course I realize that your journalists are varied in their jobs. But they basically have a shallow mind-set, feeling that their own fragmentary world-view is good enough for everybody. They really don't want their audience members to have a meaningful, coherent, and substantial picture of the world around them. Now, don't misunderstand me: I will agree that people live in their own little cages, concerned about their own little personal problems, and by and large don't want a meaningful, coherent world-view. They wouldn't know one if they saw it. I'm not one of your Lockeans or Millians of the Enlightenment who believes that mass-man is capable of ruling himself through reason.

JM: So, then, where do you come down--on the side of the journalist or on the side of the mass-person in the audience?

NM: I really don't come down, as you put it, on either side. Perhaps I am more on the side of the journalist--the person with the potential power. But what I'm simply saying is that the journalist doesn't seem to have much respect for the masses. And I'm saying that the masses generally don't deserve much respect. But, in saying this, I am not praising the journalist, who is usually a peron who doesn't have much *self*-repect, and . . .

JM: But, Nick, can a journalist have self-respect and not have respect for others?

NM: Of course. Self-respect does not necessarily mean respecting others, except perhaps in a Judeo-Christian morality. There are, naturally, some people who deserve respect in that they have earned it. To be respected by others is not a *natural right*, as John Locke might put it. I certainly don't respect everybody, and I doubt if you do either.

JM: Well, Nick, perhaps you're straying away from the subject.

NM: Perhaps I am, but I do think that the matter of respect is important. Although I said that many people don't really deserve respect, the journalist must respect them enough to cater to their desires and, perhaps, even to their needs. Said another way, the journalist must *seem* to respect the audience. For audiences are, of course, essential in journalism. So, respect--or a certain amount of it--is necessary for successful journalism--but it is generally an *instrumental* respect, one not built on merit.

JM: So you would have journalists "play games" with the public . . .

NM: Of course. Generally journalists do play their little games. They're pretty good at them. They take on roles often *irrationally* and stay with them regardless of the circumstances. They need to be more flexible, more cunning in their actions. Consistency, it has been said, is the hob-goblin of little minds.

JM: But, Nick, many critics say that journalists have no solid principles to hold on to, that they are *too* flexible in their actions...

NM: What's strange here is that, while they are tradition-bound and rather inflexible, journalists too often fall for every fad that comes along. They listen to pressure groups among the people, and they act accordingly--at least for a time, until they are temporarily led off in a different direction. But actually the public, abrasive and arrogant as some its constituent groups are, wants leadership in journalism. It wants some strong direction. But what it too often gets is a torrent of slush and mush in the form of snippets of unrelated news and unenlightened analysis. The press, if it wants to retain its power and to be "princely" instead of pathetic, had better reform its ways.

JM: Aren't you being too rough on journalists? Surely you know that there are strong, thoughtful, authentic journalists operating in my America.

NM: Of course. Always there is a remnant of courage, independence and rationality. But I'm speaking generally. Your journalists are equally as poor, weak, and inauthentic as your politicians. And that's really saying something...

JM: But, Nick, I thought you were in favor of *image*, not of real substance and authenticity. That's what I get from reading your *Prince*.

NM: You have reason to get that impression from the *Prince*. Certainly I do believe that appearances are important, that leaders (even in journalism) should create a good image. And for most people the image is more important than reality. Your whole public relations and advertising establishments are built on that belief. But let me say that *personally*--when I am not talking about pragmatics in the world as it is--I value authenticity. In my *private morality* I believe in forthrightness, honesty, integrity, and such traditional virtues. But when we talk of the real world, the practical world of successes and failures, we must shift into another morality--*a public morality*--that will help leaders and important social institutions retain their power and achieve their ends. The real leader cannot operate in his public capacity by using his private morality. He must step forward and take over, keeping the people dependent....Look at your dedicated journalist: he builds the world for audiences; he determines what they will see of the world and what they will talk about, think about...what you Americans call "agenda-setting." Some, of course, do this systematically and with specific ends in sight; others, more thoughtless and aimless, do it carelessly and chaotically. These latter journalists are just floating randomly in a journalistic sea.

JM: Since you believe that journalists should be leaders, what are some of the characteristics you feel they should have?

NM: Good minds, of course. That's first. They need to be dedicated to success, to the ends they have set for themselves. They should recognize the value of power. They should have organizational skills. They should be cunning. They should be flexible, using tactics that are best related to the situation at hand. They should learn to keep others dependent on them. They need to be decisive and action-oriented. They can't just sit around waiting for *fortuna* to direct their lives. They must make things happen, must rely on *virtù*--their own decisiveness and ingenuity. They need to be determined, persistent, and risk-taking. In short, as I said in *The Prince*, they need to be as strong as lions and as cunning as foxes.

JM: But you don't really believe that all journalists can be all of these things, do you?

NM: No I don't. Most cannot, of course. But when a journalist cannot have these characteristics, he must make people believe that he has them. He must create an image of himself as one who is courageous, powerful, and well-organized. He must *not seem* to be weak, fickle, frivolous, effeminate, cowardly, or irresolute. I discuss all of this in chapter 19 of *The Prince*.

JM: In the answer you just gave, you mention avoiding being "effeminate." You know, of course, that in modern American journalism this would not be taken seriously. We have many women as journalists, and even males who may appear effeminate. These have been, and are being, accepted into the mainstream of journalism and society.

NM: Of course, of course. I know these things, but I find it difficult to detach my answers from the context of my own day. Naturally women are effeminate; they're *expected* to be. It's their very nature. So naturally I'm not talking about them. As for homosexuals, don't be fooled. They, to be really successful even in your day, must *appear not to be effeminate*. The natural state of sexuality will never really change: men are expected to be masculine, and women are to be effeminate. That might not go over too well in your "politically correct" world, at least in public discourse, but fortunately it's not taboo in *our* world and we have the freedom to talk about such things.

JM: Would you want journalists to try to hide their timidity, cowardice, and other negative characteristics you mentioned earlier?

NM: Not if they do not need to. Why try to hide such traits if they are not interfering with the journalist's success? Of course, if they *need* to appear something they are not, then by all means they should present themselves in a false light.

JM: But do not the journalist's employers, their bosses, want journalists to be authentic, to present themselves as they are?

NM: Not at all. Editors, publishers, and other media bosses have no problem with inauthenticity. After all, they have gotten where they are by cunning and by devious methods. They have learned to live with inauthenticity, and they know their journalists are not forthright in all their activities. It's all part of the game.

JM: Do you not demean journalism when you refer to it as a game?

NM: Perhaps, but it really is a kind of game. There are rules, there are officials, there are penalties for infractions that are detected, there are objectives, there are grand strategies and tactics. And there are those who cheat and are caught and those who are not caught. There are the honest players and the dishonest ones, and there are those who are both honest and dishonest depending on the circumstances and the importance of winning.

JM: But isn't it best to play games by the rules?

NM: Journalism is a strange game in your country. It really has no solid rules, so players bow to a certain traditional mythology at times, but proceed to make up rules as they go along. The most skillful players are the journalists who are the most innovative and sly. They know just how far to deviate from the expected without suffering serious penalties. After all, in the game of journalism there are the star   players and there are the mediocrities, and there are the pluggers or mere functionaries who walk the well-worn paths with eyes straight ahead.

JM: But what is wrong with that? Aren't predictable journalists who do their jobs in a dependable manner and know how to follow orders well the kind of journalists that are extremely valuable?

NM: They are valuable, yes, just as a sword is valuable, as an instrument to use. But what is really important is the person who uses the sword for his own ends. People, journalists if you will, are valuable to the elite journalistic swordsman as instruments to be used for the swordsman's purposes.

JM: But is not this a callous way to consider most journalists--as instruments? Did not Kant say that we should never use persons as means, but always as ends?

NM: Kant was Kant. I am Machiavelli. What he says simply is a reflection of the fact that he did not really live in the real pragmatic world. He was the prototype of the unrealistic monkish philosopher that spouts concepts from an experiential vacuum. But as to your basic question, I'd say that it is not really callous to treat journalists as instruments. The good swordsman has great respect, even love, for his sword. He takes care of it. He favors the sturdy and dependable sword so that it will serve him well in his mission.

JM: What you seem to be saying is that most journalists are to be used by other more powerful journalists and that this is all right.

NM: Correct. It is quite natural for some to use and others to be used.

That is the way of the world, and that's the way it will always be. This does not mean that I am *against* the journalist who is used or that I think him somehow less than human. Not at all. He is just in a different role, a perfectly reasonable role, a necessary role in the human enterprise of journalism. We cannot all be bosses. We cannot all have equal power and goals. Some must lead, and some must follow. Some must see the big picture, deal with the strategies, and shake the society; others must serve as instruments for the powerful leaders.

JM: But most of our journalists and aspiring journalists have no such grand illusions as to grand schemes. They simply want to inform the people, do some small bit in helping society, and work for and with other people. What is wrong with that?

NM: Nothing at all is wrong with that. In fact, it is good that there are such persons who are satisfied to be virtually powerless. They make good functionaries and followers. They are essential in the game of journalism. Not everyone can drive the coach; most must be passengers.

JM: But you seem to think that journalists should seek power and be leaders, and that they should strive to attain this status by any means that works.

NM: Not at all. I am in favor of the strong-willed, the intelligent, the cunning, and the dedicated reaching the positions of power. Not everyone. As I have just said, there must be the followers, the instruments in the hands of the powerful. The press as a total institution may be *princely* in the sense of being powerful and leading society, but this does not mean that every journalist is a prince.

JM: I know it is about time to stop, Nick. So, in conclusion, could you summarize briefly your ideal profile of a good journalist?

NM: Briefly? I'll try. The journalist is not a weakling. He is dedicated to success. He believes in rational self-interest, in individualism (for himself at least), in power, in vision, courage, and dedication. He is a person of pride, of social transcendence, of leadership. He must be practical, competitive, ambitious, and have that "bottom-line," winner-take-all spirit. After all, American journalism, as I understand it, sees itself as a Prince that legitimately lords it over other institutions and seeks to strike fear into the hearts of even elected officials. Remember that I am talking about the strong-willed journalist who desires power--the "princely" journalist who is more than a mere functionary. Shall I continue talking about this journalist?

JM: Please do.

NM: This journalist does not seek love, but respect. And he gets this from exercising power. He should be the guiding light of the people, the conscience and royal spokesman for the nation. His journalism is protected by your Royal Charter's very first amendment. He should flaunt his rights and power at every opportunity, and never be satisfied with any kind of restriction on his power. He should make sure that the people recognize his status as representative of the Press, the real Prince of your modern society. And, finally, he must determine never to submit to those who feel they know more about journalism than he does, and he must fight all efforts to make him conform to some social concept of "responsibility." Let me say that journalism has the power; therefore journalism has the freedom...and this freedom, of course, includes the right to seek one's own self-interest and to act in any journalistic way one chooses. These are some of my general observations about the journalist. I'm sure we shall have opportunity to elaborate further on the subject later.

JM: Indeed you shall, Nick. Thank you for your remarks. I'll see you again tomorrow when we'll talk about the mission of the media.

Chapter 4

Mission

[August 4, 1520]

NM: *Buon Giorno.* And how are you this rainy morning?

JM: Not bad, Nick. Please forgive my muddy feet; your front walkway is almost under water. Today I hope that we can continue our discussion about journalists--focusing this time on their purpose, their function, their mission.

NM: Fine.

JM: You have said in *The Prince* that nobles cannot be trusted unless their fortunes are tied to those of the Prince. Would you say this is also true with reporters and other journalists--in respect to their relationship to editors and publishers?

NM: But naturally. Reporters are to editors as nobles are to princes. Individuals tend to go their own directions unless they see common benefits in cooperative action. This is why journalistic freedom, carried very far, is counterproductive in a medium of mass communication. So we'll talk more of freedom in another interview, I understand. But let me get to some thoughts about journalistic mission.

JM: Please do. Sorry I got off the subject with that question.

NM: Actually there is no *one* mission for journalism. There are many missions. But basic to all is *success*; that is the central mission, the underlying *raison d'etre*. Staying viable, achieving purposes, making money, gaining power. Also journalism is in the *image business*. Creating images is a prime function--images of the medium itself, of the management, of the people and world it purports to describe...

JM: But where does *success* come in here? What kind of image connotes success on the part of journalism?

NM: The achievement of the *desired* image or end is what I mean by successful journalism. If I am the editor, I have in mind an image I want people to have of whatever I am writing about. If I'm successful, I'll achieve that. If I want to make money and do so, then I am successful. If I can achieve *all* my desires, then I am *very* successful. Editors and reporters, in straining reality through their perceptions, create their own reality and pass it on as the reality for others.

JM: Well, Nick, let's get off this subject now, for as I've told you, we'll deal with the subject of objectivity in journalism later.

NM: That's fine, but I just wanted to say that the creation of journalistic reality is *a* primary mission of journalism.

JM: What would you say is *the* primary mission of journalism?

NM: Social control. No doubt about it: the institution of journalism is a controlling one. It exists to shape society, to impact history, and to use its power to keep power in the hands of its allies. By and large, journalism is a power-machine that runs society just as one of your dynamos runs an electrical network.

JM: Please elaborate on that.

NM: A certain Lord Acton of England is said to have said that power corrupts and that absolute power corrupts absolutely. This is a ridiculous saying. What I say is that a *lack of power* corrupts, for there is nothing or nobody as pitifully impotent as when there is no power. Of course, my definition of "corrupt" is somewhat different. I think of corruption as the state of being powerless or impotent--of not being able to achieve ends, of always being frustrated, of being unable or unwilling to do what is necessary to succeed. As you probably know, the easiest person to corrupt is that person who is powerless, and therefore willing to submit to the will of another in hopes to better his condition.

JM: But can't an editor, for example, be corrupt in the very process of using his power to bring others to abide by his will?

NM: Perhaps by your usual definition of corrupt, yes. But not as I see it. The editor is the editor; the publisher is the publisher. They are leaders, and as such, are expected to be willful, and thus powerful. They must be strong and determined, and contrary to the thrust of your question, the use of power by an editor can never be corrupt--even if the results do not please everyone. It is when the editor is passive, or indecisive, or too moderate that corruption spreads throughout the whole journalistic enterprise. It is then that idle and harmful gossip spreads like a cancer; it is then that the workers begin to feel that *they* should have more say; it is then that the leader's power begins to drain from him and the whole enterprise founders on the rocks of indecision and a false sense of the reasonableness of the collective will.

JM: What do you mean by the "collective will"?

NM: The idea that everybody is the leader. The collectivization of the idea of leadership is a false one, and, I might add, a very dangerous one for the institution. Leadership in journalism, as in any other area, comes, or should come, from the top. It does not grow like poppies from the flat soil of the common worker. All the sailors on the ship may have their little jobs to do, but it is the captain who must steer the ship. Poor is the powerless, impotent captain who permits a hundred hands to push and tug at the wheel! And can you guess where the ship, under such collectivized steering, would go?

JM: But don't you believe in cooperation in journalism?

NM: Naturally. But I do not believe in cooperation and collective effort in leadership. And when journalistic leaders try to share their leadership with their audiences, that is really sad. Leading a newspaper, for example, is not a democratic enterprise; it is an elite enterprise.

JM: But, back to journalistic mission. Wouldn't you say that the main mission of journalism is to provide credible and useful information on the basis of which the public can act responsibly for the good of all?

NM: You sound like John Stuart Mill, John Dewey, Robert Hutchins, John Rawls--some people you are familiar with. These are persons who, along with myriads of sentimentalists, dwell in that mystical city of Altruria.

JM: Are you really so opposed to altruism, to thinking about public good, public service, and journalism's utilitarian purpose?

NM: I am opposed to sentimental, unrealistic journalism, yes. Journalism must, first of all, be egocentric. It must care for itself; it must expand its power-base and protect itself against encroachments from the State and from the people. Journalism, as I see it, especially in your country, is a private enterprise striving to expand its power and its profits. Period. That's its main concern. Now, if it takes some "public service," some slight bending to the public taste, to expand power and profits, then so be it. Expediency and compromise for the purpose of success is always justified. But journalists should remember that this is *secondary*, not primary. What is primary is self-interest, self-growth, self-enhancement, self-control, and success.

JM: But is not a journalism that conforms to your pattern devoid of any social-consciousness, any conscience if you will?

NM: Not at all. My kind of journalism definitely is conscious of society. If it weren't, it could not be the pragmatic, self-achieving enterprise I want it to be. A journalism that is not aware of society, of its audiences, is really not a journalism at all. Journalism can be socially conscious without being dominated or directed by society. My kind of journalism is knowledgeable of society, is conscious of society *so that it can use society to its own ends.* My basic journalistic question is this: How can I manipulate society for my own ends while giving the impression that I care about, am thinking about, society's ends?

JM: But isn't that a very arrogant, elitist, self-righteous attitude? Surely you can't fool the people very long with such a cynical attitude.

NM: Sure, it is a self-righteous, self-centered attitude. It is also a very pragmatic one. Do not your journalists in America go about singing paeans to "the people's right to know" while determining at every turn what the people will and will not know? Do not they dedicate themselves to a pluralistic journalism while conforming to a business-oriented monolithic corporate perspective? Do not your journalists emit shouts of indignation every time someone suggests that certain of their messages are socially harmful? Do not your journalists regularly show their self-centeredness by wrapping themselves in First Amendment protection whenever their actions are challenged? Actually, *my* concept of journalism is not too far removed from that of America at the end of the 20th century. Your journalists, unless they are hypocritical (which, of course, they have every right to be) should agree with my concept of journalism which you have called "cynical." I prefer the world "realistic," of course.

JM: But can you fool the people very long with this attitude that you prefer to call "realistic"?

NM: The people are easy to fool. In fact, they want to be fooled. It is only a handful of thoughtful people, intellectuals if you like, who hate the thought of being fooled. But even they are fooled, and quite often. The people in general...they are fooled most of the time. They have so little information, and they have no real inclination to get it. They will believe almost anything, or if they don't believe it or have doubts about it, they don't have the persistence, the energy, or the real desire to seek the true facts. Yes, I'd say they are rather easily fooled, and that they often confuse the journalist's interest with their own.

JM: Would you try to wrap up what you have said about journalism's mission thus far, Nick?

NM: I'm not really good at doing that. I realize that you journalists like to capsulize everything, to offer compact summaries, and the like. That's very hard for us Florentines. But I'll try, although I may stray away into other areas. Journalism's main mission is to wield power, to influence society, to shape society, to determine what kind of government exists...and, above all, to garner increasing power and to use it according to its own institutional and editorial self-determination. Journalism is not simply an instrument, a plaything, for the people. It is a self-defined, egocentric institution that leads and does not follow, except on occasion when it is expedient for it to do so. Its mission is to protect itself, to grow, to gain power, to use power for its own ends. But, as I have said, it often will create the image of a socially concerned institution. Although it is motivated by egoism, it creates the illusion of altruism. Although it is obsessed by its freedom, it sets about to create the illusion of social responsibility. It talks much about its social functions of informing, analyzing, and educating; but it concentrates on entertaining and propagandizing. Is mission is not to make more discerning citizens; rather its mission is to solidify its own power by dulling the intellect of the citizens. It does this by offering them non-nutritious desserts, by luring them into playful pastures, by causing them to feel rather than think, and by providing them with bits and pieces of reality so that they will know only a world of discontinuity and stereotypes. Such journalism is a placebo for the masses--or, if you prefer, such journalism is an "opiate" for people. Journalism, not God, creates for the people their heaven and their earth.

JM: Well, Nick, let me interrupt here. I do think you have rather clearly given your idea of journalism's mission. Not many journalists in my country in my day will agree with it, however. But it is interesting...

NM: Oh, they will agree with it. That is if they have not lost all contact with honesty and reality. They may not *say* that they agree with it. And that's all right...to be expected. Why would they admit publicly that they are basically ego-centric and power-driven? They must maintain the image of a socially concerned, truth-seeking institution motivated mainly by altruism. And I'm not sure we should abruptly leave this point. It is very important in a discussion of mission.

JM: All right, Nick. We'll continue with this a little longer. The idea, though, of journalism creating a world for people seems a little farfetched to me. Are you not giving the mass media too much credit, or blame, for the state of society?

NM: I think not.   Journalism and its handmaidens, the so-called entertainment messages of the media--have a very great impact on people's concerns, interests, perspectives, and opinions. As some of your scholars say, they "set the agenda" really for social concern and action. And, as I have said, I think this is basically the mission of journalism. Most journalists are lured into journalism because they perceive it as a field of social power, a place where they can take society in a given direction, where they can have some leverage in social engineering.

JM: But aren't you negating the intelligence of the mass media audiences, and deprecating the individual decision-making potential of the audience member?

NM: Of course not. Journalism dominates public thinking. Journalism subsumes the individual and paints the picture of the world that either pleases or nauseates the audience. It is almost impossible for an audience to think about politics, economics, art, literature or anything else without depending on basic guidance from journalists. This is not to say that a certain audience member may not disagree with a perspective received from the media, but it does mean that it is not easy to escape it. And, of course, this audience member must have other media-imposed information on which to base a disagreement. And, naturally, all such journalism is partial and inadequate for thorough understanding. The journalist's mission is clear: it is to shape reality into images and stereotypes which are relatively simple and easy to grasp.

JM: How then can a citizen get information, perspectives, and the like that are adequate and dependable for the understanding of reality?

NM: Well, actually he cannot ever get what he needs. But he can receive, of course, more depth and insightful perspective than he might get from journalism. For instance, he can read books and talk with wise people. But even there, he is trapped by the insufficiency of background and interpretation. Books are so plentiful and, like journalism, so biased that the poor reality-seeker is helpless in the face of this pluralism of superficiality.

JM: So what does the citizen do?

NM: What he does is to resign himself to living in the pseudo-world of journalism, where images are simplified and where information snippets are few enough so as not to confuse or overwhelm. This is why journalism as an institutionalized operation is so powerful: because people *must*, in most cases, depend on it for their basic information and opinions.

JM: But why don't they read more books and talk with more wise persons?

NM: Too much effort required. And, as I said, too difficult to find the *right* books. And, as for talking with wise persons, this is not easy either. In the first place, there are not many such persons and when they might be found they are not anxious to talk with the seeker. In fact, one trait of the wise person is that he is not loquacious. Thinking, meditation, and action are far more important. One important trait of a wise person is that he does not want to waste his time talking about very complex issues with the others.

JM: But you suggested books, and wise persons are good sources for a person seeking information and perspectives that cannot be obtained from journalism.

NM: Yes, I know, but I still see such knowledge-seeking as very difficult. Of course, the persistent person will get closer to reality-knowledge and wisdom than will the timid and lazy person. And, of course, there are wise people who are, at least at times, quite loquacious, for example: *me.* You are talking with me, and you are learning much that you could not find in journalism. But it is not easy. Few people have managed to have such talks as you are having with me.

JM: And I appreciate your talking with me very much. But we are talking about the mission of journalism. You seem to think that the mission is to dupe the people, to lead them in certain directions, to withhold much truth from them, and in general to manipulate them. Is that right?

NM: Essentially so. The mission of journalism is to create a world of images for the people--a world that feeds upon itself, that stimulates further journalistic stimulation, further abstraction, further and simpler distortions. The ultimate mission: the ushering of vast audiences into a media-world that is unreal but which seems real.

JM: But isn't this harmful to the people?

NM: I doubt it. Most people have no desire to confront reality and complexity. They thrive on simplicity. They wouldn't know what to do with the truth if they had it. If journalism didn't program the people, they would be programmed by very limited personal contacts and experiences. It may well be that they are better off with the simple worldview of journalism than they would be with their own individual direct and personal experiential confrontation of reality. Journalism defines and structures the world for them; it gives them a certain comfort in the face of a frightening and all-encompassing universe.

JM: Then you are saying that journalism is a good thing for people?

NM: Yes, I am. In fact, you might say that journalism's *mission* is facilitated by a basic desire for simplification on the part of the masses. The audiences almost *demand* that journalists construct their world for them.

JM: I think, Nick, that with that we had better stop today. You're losing me here and there with some of your last remarks. Perhaps we'll come back to some of this.

NM: I hope we shall, for this is very interesting to me.

JM: Well, I'll say good-bye for now. I know you plan to meet with some of your friends at the tavern and talk about more mundane things. I appreciate your comments today about journalism's mission. Many thanks. I'll get my coat and umbrella and brave the elements outside. This must be an unusually rainy August. Farewell for now.

[Machiavelli rose, nodded as I made my last remark, walked to the window, and looked out at the rain. I put on my coat, took up my umbrella, and left by the front door, leaving my interviewee standing silently at the window watching me as I trudged toward the road fronting the house.]

Chapter 5

Power

[August 5, 1520]

NM: Come in *signore*. Let us get started. I'm glad you came today instead of tomorrow. I must go over to Florence in the morning to confer with University officials about the new post I'll take up in about three months. On November 1, I think.

JM: And what post is that?

NM: I'll be officially known as "historiographer of the republic." I'll only get a rather small stipend for that but, fortunately, I can be employed in other ways also.   And very soon I shall begin writing a discourse on the organization of Florence after Duke Lorenzo's death. But, then, you are not interested in all this.

JM: It's very interesting, sir, but I do want us to deal with a very important subject today. I hope you will talk about one of your favorite topics, *power*, and how it relates to journalism. In my country in my times journalists talk much about their importance in limiting power of the big social institutions, of dangerous fanatics, and especially of governmental officials.

NM: Yes, of course, I am interested in power. In fact, power is the key to my whole philosophy of politics, and, I might add, by extension, to my thoughts about journalism. Your question leads me to assume that your journalists think they are suspicious of, and perhaps, afraid of, power. Why else would they want to limit government power, for instance? Well, I don't subscribe to that premise. Your journalists are as power-hungry as the government people; in fact, they relish the power they have in curbing government's power.

JM: But, Nick, our journalists don't see themselves as power-seekers or as power-brokers. They see themselves as checks on power, as mediating forces in the corruptive attempts by social institutions to harness power.

NM: That may well be what they say. But they really know better. They are dedicated to power, to getting it and keeping it, even to expanding it. I know about their self-concept as a "fourth branch of government." Is that not a *power* concept? And do not they see their power potential when they wrap themselves in your First Amendment freedom guarantee? And are they not "adversaries" of government, with all the power ramifications that entails? No, I doubt very much that your journalists scorn power.

JM: But they say very little, if anything, about it . . .

NM: Why should they? There is no need to *talk* about power. Just get it, keep it, and expand it. And your press system does this very well, indeed. Nobody can lay a hand on your journalists; they are protected; they always have the last word; they can paint the world as *they* want it to be; they can push and shove and invade privacy; they can create stereotypes; they can exaggerate and they can ignore. In fact, they can make reality conform to their visions and desires. Now, that's real power.

JM: But our press quite often does not take on government; it treats powerful   politicians with sympathy and dignity, and there is no overt striving for power on the part of most journaists I know . . .

NM: You're quite right. And why should the press flaunt its power at every opportunity? Part of power is resisting its use on occasion. As I have said many times, it is often necessary, and smart, to avoid   offending powerful patrons and essential social agencies. The government and the people, of course, are two such groups. But having said that, I can assure you that the press uses its power whenever it wants to, and sometimes it backfires, and for short periods your journalists enjoy very little public support.

JM: But how can you say that our journalists often enjoy little support? People, even government officials, keep reading the newspapers and watching television for their news.

NM: The obvious answer to that is that your press is the only game in town, as you say. Sure the people keep getting their news from your press. Where else can they turn? Maybe to your Internet, but it is still pretty much in its infancy and, besides, it has very little credibility as I understand it. At present this almost monopoly of public information is one of the prime reasons for the press's great power.

JM: Let me turn to another aspect of this topic. Assuming the press has, and desires, power: is that good or bad?

NM: Good or bad? I'm never sure what people mean when they use those terms. Let me say this: I certainly have nothing against loving power, and exercising it. Therefore, there is nothing wrong with journalists having power. The question with power is really this: If I have it, am I using it? And, more importantly, am I using it successfully?

JM: What do you mean by using it "successfully"?

NM: I mean achieving my predetermined ends. Am I making use of my power in such a way as to make my program or plan successful? Am I as a journalist harnessing my power to my objective so as to attain my desired ends? That is the basic power question for the journalist.

JM: Do you mean that journalists should use their power to achieve their own selfish purposes? Isn't that unethical?

NM: You already know my feeling about that, and since we're going to discuss ethics later this month, I will simply repeat my basic tenet that one must use power to get desired results. For what other purpose would a person want to use power?

JM: Then, you would say that there is nothing wrong with a journalism that is powerful, in the sense of having the capacity to achieve its purposes?

NM: That is exactly right. I would definitely say that. Your American press is often criticized by those who see it as too negative, too haughty, too elitist, too smug, too callous, too sensational, too monopolistic, or too-this-or-that. But at the base of all this criticism is an envy of power. If your press were not powerful, then all these perceived "sins" could be ignored, or laughed off. This is why I say that your press should be proud of its power and relish the criticism that it receives.

JM: But will not such "pride"--or arrogance, if you will--lead to the public's loss of faith in the press? Will not such a selfish demeanor on the part of journalism endanger its own success and future?

NM: That, of course, is possible...if the press goes too far and alienates too many people--and too many constituencies with power. But if your press is wise, and I think it is generally, it will not go beyond the limits of reasoned pragmatism. It will use its power moderately, in the main. It will alienate some, of course; it will even antagonize important and powerful elements in the society--but it must simply make sure that such elements are scattered and unrelated enough so as not to pose any kind of organized antagonistic Power-Bloc. And this is not too difficult for your press; in fact it does this very effectively. What does it matter that your journalists insult this person or that person, that they distort a story or two each day, that they misquote a few people here and there? So what? All this will not even be detected by many audience members and will be quickly forgotten by those few who do notice these press exploits. Journalists can get by with shabby work, with making mistakes, with distortion and censorship very easily.

JM: But journalists must have credibility. They must be trusted by the people. . .

NM: Most people, in most circumstances will trust your journalists. That's my point. Journalism is safe from public harm because of basic and general public ignorance. How can the people generally mistrust the press when they know almost nothing except what the press tells them? And, as I have said, what alternative source of information do the people have? In a sense the people *have to* trust the press. And they generally do--although admittedly among many thoughtful people there is a basic suspicion of, or skepticism regarding, the accuracy and comprehensiveness of the stories they receive from the press.

JM: And you see all this related to the press's power?

NM: Exactly. Your journalism is legally protected; it is pluralistically accurate and inaccurate, thorough and superficial, careful and careless, serious and flippant, socially helpful and socially harmful, benevolent and mean-spirited. In short, your journalism is largely beyond the law and, at the same time, beyond your prized "marketplace" controls. This is power with a capital "P." Since your press has a virtual monopoly on public information, and since it cannot easily be restrained by your legal system, and since it has no social institution to keep a watch on its multitudinous activities, it is the most powerful enterprise in your country.

JM: Well, Nick, I wish we could continue with this, but I'm sure you'll say more about this later. But it is getting late, and I know you usually go down to the tavern to talk with your friends. But before I go, I would like to have you pinpoint your view of journalism in my country in respect to power.

NM: Power is meant to be used. Much of your press does not use the great power it possesses. What a waste! And many of your journalists go about their days functioning as senseless robots, uttering shibboleths about their Constitutional freedom, but showing no enterprise and courage-- showing no inclination to use the great power that they have. There seems to be no policy or reason for most of the journalism in your country: therefore there is a kind of "power-vacuum" created by journalism's inaction, by the press's inability to formulate a clearly defined mission and use its power to achieve it. Segments of your press, of course, are power-conscious and do set goals to which powerful means are applied. But, I'm afraid that most of your press fritters its power away in the daily tedium of unsystemitized activity signifying nothing but routine busy-ness.

JM: Now, for a last question. Would you, in light of what you hve said, like to see the American press become more powerful--or use its power more effectively?

NM: Yes I would. That is, if the American press knows what it wants to achieve. As I have said, it appears to me that your journalism really has no consistent, definitive objective. It is so splintered and diffused in philosophy that it seems to really be going nowhere except into the land of greater and greater profits. And, of course, wealth relates very much to power, but it does not really get at changing public attitudes and directions. That's the kind of power I'm mainly concerned about. Your press doesn't seem to agree on much--except, possibly making profits--and this is one reason its power is muted. Your press can't even come up with a common definition of "news." It is uncertain as to whether it can be "objective" or whether it can be fair. So, I would say, in conclusion--and I really must be going--that if your journalism gets its conceptual house in order and knows what it wants to do, I would indeed like to see it get to be more powerful. Impact, social potency, effectiveness--yes, all of these are ingredients of, and results of, power. Perhaps we can say that power is the machine that runs conceptual journalism, but at present there is the power but little conceptual journalism to run.

JM: I wish we had more time today, for I think you have short-changed American journalism so far as its institutional concept is concerned. There is considerable agreement among journalists about journalism's basic concepts, but I will admit that there is much confusion, too.

NM: Sorry we can't talk more about this, but I'll try to get into it in a later interview.

JM: Well, thank you, Nick. You have been very kind. We'll talk again day after tomorrow.

Chapter 6

Freedom

[August 7, 1520]

JM: Good morning, Nick. As you know, we are to talk about freedom of
the press today. Press freedom is a most important tenet in America. I would
like to hear your ideas concerning this subject. To get started, admittedly in
a rather prosaic way, let me put this to you: How would you define "press
freedom"?

NM: This is really too large a question to get us started. Perhaps by the
time we have finished today, I will have answered it to some extent. Press
freedom means just what a certain party wants it to mean at any particular
time.   I'm not too concerned, really, with freedom of any kind if it is
unrelated to power. As I have said elsewhere, power really determines
freedom: he who has the power has the freedom.

JM: But what about *press* freedom? Often a newspaper, for example, has
very little power. Would you say that it should therefore not have freedom?

NM: All institutions in society have *some* power. Thus a newspaper with
some power will have some freedom. Nobody has complete freedom in a
society--because, of course, there is no absolute power. A society implies
limited freedom; all parties must give up certain freedoms in order to
function as a social unit--or as a state. Therefore, I would say that your
newspaper will have some freedom. And as its power increases, so will its
freedom.

JM: But it is difficult to see that some newspapers have *any* real power in
society.

NM: Oh, but they do. The problem is that their leaders and functionaries don't use the power they have. Power--and with it, freedom--is there, but most often it is hardly used--or not used at all.

JM: But you are not dealing with the thrust of my question as to what the place of press freedom is. Are you for it or against it?

NM: I am neither for nor against it. I simply recognize that it, in certain degrees, exists. In America, your press seems to have a considerable degree of it--coming from tradition and from your national constitution. You prize it because you have it. And, then, you *don't* prize it--and again, this is because you have it.

JM: What do you mean?

NM: You don't really appreciate it, although you talk a lot about it. You take it for granted, and therefore you don't use it. If you didn't have it--or much of it--you would appreciate it more, and you would use it more. Now, as to whether it is good or bad, I must say that such a question always disturbs me. Freedom is sometimes good and sometimes bad. It depends on circumstances or context of its use and whether or not it is being used pragmatically.

JM: I hate to say it, but I don't understand that last statement.

NM: Well, it is enough to say here that my freedom is good for me, and possibly bad for you. And if I am using my freedom to achieve egoistic ends, you very well may not think it's good. But if I am using my freedom to help you, you may very well commend me and like my freedom.

JM: So, freedom is sometimes good and sometimes bad. I can accept that. But would you say a little more about it?

NM: Well, freedom is good--for the press, for example--if it is used to expand power. It is bad, on the other hand, when it causes a social or state reaction that endangers or narrows press power. So how can I really say that it is good or bad? Freedom depends on how it is used--or *if* it is used pragmatically or in a non-productive manner. Freedom unused or chaotically used is either valueless or anarchic. Being a strong proponent of discipline and of social direction, I am naturally opposed to dormant or aimless freedom.

JM: But is relating freedom to power, as you have done, fair to the person who needs freedom for personal satisfaction? He or she has no power to speak of, but does justice not require that he or she have freedom?

NM: No. Justice does not require that. After all, justice is nothing more than the name given by men of power to any actions they enjoin their subjects to conduct. What is just is what is for the interest of the stronger, the most powerful. Right and wrong, just and unjust: these concepts have no meaning outside the limits of power.

JM: You sound like...what was his name? Oh, yes: Thrasymachus, I think it was. He said virtually what you are saying when he was arguing with Socrates in ancient Athens.

NM: Right you are! Thrasymachus is one of my heroes and intellectual forebears. I'm surprised that you see the similarity between his ideas and mine. You may recall that Thrasymachus favored a leader or ruler who was a despot (or as the Greeks said, a tyrant), a man who had the power and the will to do good to himself and his friends and to handle his enemies or competitors with what is really "justice."

JM: But didn't Socrates demolish the arguments of Thrasymachus in the first book of Plato's *Republic*?

NM: Not at all. Socrates, in his usual slick manner of argument, and urged on by the sycophants who surrounded him, *seemed* to get the better of Thrasymachus. But actually history has proven Socrates wrong. Power, used by the strongest, always triumphs in the real, pragmatic world. Socrates, like so many throughout history, lived in a fool's paradise--in a false, intellectualized world of what I call "intellectual mysticism" where verbal play seems more important that reality. Socrates was critical of "sophists," but was a leading exponent himself of such verbal manipulators. And Plato...Plato was probably history's best example of this kind of romanticized mysticism, believing that the real world, the world of actuality and objectivity, is no more than a reflection of some "ideal" world. What hogwash! Oh yes, we use that saying, too. First used down south of Rome, I think, by a farmer named Guillici.

JM: But my world remembers Socrates and Plato and hardly knows anything about Thrasymachus--most of us have probably never even heard his name.

NM: More the pity! Thrasymachus speaks for the ages, for the realistic social situation everywhere. A strong, discerning and hard-minded pragmatist was Thrasymachus, one that I consider at the forefront of historical evolution.

JM: But, Nick, you seem to value freedom only as it enhances power, or symbolizes power. Is that not so?

NM: You might say that. But perhaps I should modify that somewhat. I am in favor of freedom that enhances *my* power, not just anyone's power. For example, if I am a governmental leader, I would not like to see the press get more freedom. I would want to enhance my power--government power-- and therefore I would be concerned about freedom and power, but not freedom and power for everybody.

JM: But this sounds very selfish. You support freedom but not for all-- only for yourself and your institution. Is not this a very antisocial and narrow view of freedom?

NM: Freedom for all is anarchy. Certainly I don't want freedom for all-- unless, of course, everybody is capable of achieving enough power to deserve such freedom. And that will never happen. What I want is freedom for the deserving, for the capable, for the strong, for the intelligent, for those who know how to use it.

JM: But who is to say that certain parts of the press are deserving and intelligent enough to have freedom?

NM: Nobody has to *say* it. History will prove it; some media will remain viable, even grow; others will vegetate, even die. The strongest will survive; the weakest will die. And the strongest here, I must add, are not necessarily those that provide the highest quality information. They are those which can adapt to the realities of life at a particular time. They are those who can supply what is demanded--or wanted by a fickle public. These survivors of the press are the expedient, the practical, and the realistic.

JM: You are supporting the idea of the survival of the fittest?

NM: I am supporting, really, the survival of the realistic, the practical, and the adaptable. Some media, for instance, want to play by idealistic, esoteric rules having to do with some kind of "fairness" principle; they will follow these principles to their very demise. Other media have more realistic aspirations: they want to survive; they want to achieve their ends; they will sacrifice personal moral tenets to life and power. In adapting, they persevere. In compromising, they persist. In bonding--even breaking social norms when necessary--they grow. They are the strong-willed media, the powerful media, the ones that are willing to sacrifice the conventional morality to the morality of life, of growth, of influence, of power.

JM: You sound much like Nietzsche when he describes his "Overman" and makes his distinction between "master-morality" and "slave-morality."

NM: Perhaps so. But it would be more accurate to say that he sounds more like me, since I predated him by some three centuries. Actually I sound more like old Thrasymachus--we discussed him earlier. I have a very warm place in my heart--oh, yes, I have one--for old Thrasymachus. I'm not so sure about Nietzsche; he talked tough, but was basically a whiner and a weakling.

JM: Well, let's get back to freedom. In America we think press freedom will help us come up with the truth; therefore it has a utilitarian basis--as you might say, a pragmatic basis. But at the same time many of us subscribe to John Locke's idea that freedom of expression is a natural right. How do you feel about these two rationales for press freedom?

NM: I would be more prone to subscribe to the former--that freedom is instrumental or utilitist, as John Stuart Mill believed. Certainly I cannot believe that freedom is a "natural right." This would negate the whole idea of socialization with its imposition of authorities. However, I must say that I am dubious about press freedom bringing truth to light. More often, I think, maximum press freedom does the exact opposite--it tends to hide truth under many layers of contradictory and interpretive information. And it gives solace to propagandists of every stripe. Yes, freedom is utilitarian--I prefer the word "utilitist," but only in the sense of permitting the powerful to become more powerful.

JM: But, Nick, won't a free press give truth the best chance by exposing a wide variety of information--and by calling the hand of the propagandist?

NM: Not necessarily. How does the poor citizen know what to believe out of this barrage of variable data flooding in on him? It could well be that the truth or part of it is, in fact, out there in the press messages somewhere--but how does the audience member know where to find it or to recognize it as truth when he thinks he has found it? The press knows that it does not have the truth. It simply has small portions of it...and portions of falsity also...and it is not certain itself which is which. Pity the poor audience member who thinks the truth will emerge from such a situation!

JM: You sound as if you're really concerned about the person you call "the poor audience member."

NM: Well, that was a rhetorical reference, strictly for the purpose of making my point about truth winning out. Actually I don't care much for the audience--except as the audience can help me achieve my ends. And, besides, I care little about the audience knowing the truth--especially about me and my tactics for achieving my end.

JM: I am beginning to get the feeling that you are not a firm supporter of press freedom. Am I right?

NM: Here we go again. Some antics with semantics. I am, in truth, a firm supporter of press freedom and at the same time I am not a firm supporter. If I put myself into the shoes of the journalist, then I support the concept. If I put myself into the shoes of the governmental official, then I am not a supporter of the concept. Favoring something or not favoring something is relative. Relative to vested interest, mainly. But also relative to time, place, and circumstance.

JM: So you don't see press freedom as an absolute benefit?

NM: No I don't. There are really no absolutes--except the absolute superiority of dominance of power over weakness. But, of course, we could get into deep semantic waters here--talking about what we mean by "power" and "weakness."

JM: So let's get back to press freedom.

NM: I didn't know we had left it. But I'll continue. What I'm saying really is that the press must earn its freedom. It must constantly use it to force back the restrictions that almost everyone is trying to use against it. Push, push, push. That's what must be done by the press. Passive freedom atrophies, even in the most liberal or unrestrained societies. Actually, all societies have more press freedom than they think they have...in other words they have more than they really use.

JM: It is easy for you to say these things but it would be more difficult if you had to face the consequences of going too far in your use of freedom. And isn't this especially true in authoritarian countries?

NM: Of course it is harder to use freedom in authoritarian regimes. That is inherent in the term "authoritarian regime." What the British philosopher of your day, Isaiah Berlin, has termed "negative freedom" is largely absent in such regimes. But even in such restrictive situations there is some room for "positive freedom"--freedom to act--and I might add that in many more cases than you would think, it can be used without serious consequences. It just takes will, courage, and persistence. And, of course, a little sophistication and cunning in *how* it is used. Unfortunately, sophistication and cunning--and especially courage--are not in great supply among journalists.

JM: Are you implying in all this, Nick, that the use of freedom by journalists generally is a good thing?

NM: Again, it depends on the perspective you have. If I am a journalist wanting to use freedom to accomplish my ends, then it is a good thing. If I am a government official wanting to keep the journalist in his predictable conformist mode, then for *me* his use of freedom is *not* good. And, I might add, that for many journalists any use of freedom is frightening and even traumatic.

JM: Why would that be?

NM: Because many, maybe most, journalists don't want to use freedom. They are satisfied to follow orders, do the expected, and keep out of as many decision making areas as possible.

JM: But I have never heard a single journalist say he or she did not want freedom.

NM: I'm sure you haven't. Certainly the journalist wouldn't say it, for freedom is what a journalist in your country is supposed to cherish. But saying you want freedom and saying you want *to use* freedom are two different things. And anyway, the individual journalist, as I have said, is really not in the position to have much freedom even if he wants it. It is the owner or one of his chief minions in a leadership position that really has the freedom. The average journalist has the freedom to gripe and to leave for another job. He usually does much of the first, and seldom resorts to the second alternative.

JM: But you have said that this journalist *can* use more freedom than he or she does.

NM: That is correct. Even in the virtually powerless situation in which most journalists find themselves, they can exercise their freedom to a greater degree than they do. Fear, complacency, or simple inertia keep them from venturing into areas of possible action. In a way it is a sad thing that freedom largely goes unused. But then, looked at another way it is a good thing: too many strong-willed, freedom-seeking journalists might result in even greater chaotic, even nihilistic, journalism. But we don't need to worry--few journalists will rock the journalistic boat with their freedom demands. The very few will have the freedom, and also the power.

JM: You seem to be satisfied with this general scarcity of freedom among journalists.

NM: Yes, I am satisfied. But it is a natural situation. In any enterprise, there are few who lead and many who follow. Think of the chaos that results from an opposite system. Freedom is a banner waved by timid souls to boost their spirits as they march to the drumbeat of the more powerful.

JM: That sounds good, Nick. But what about freedom used by the powerful themselves?

NM: Of course, freedom used by the powerful and the courageous is quite different.

JM: How so?

NM: For them it is more than a banner; it is a fact, an unvoiced, unheralded reality. And as freedom is accompanied automatically by power, together they can sweep everything aside that tends to impede them. It is a mighty combination, one that every true leader understands.

JM: Many pressures exist today in my country to curb press freedom, for the critics maintain that journalism has become too superficial, careless, irresponsible, and freedom has deteriorated into no more than license. What do you think of that?

NM: Most of this criticism of the media is really coming from your new communitarians found mainly in your universities, but to some degree in the press itself. Calls to make the press more responsible have always indicated a basic dissatisfaction with freedom and a desire for more direction. Journalists must stand up against such arrogant calls for control. They must recognize that "responsible journalism" is best determined in a pluralistic manner by a large number of journalistic voices. No group of ordinary citizens or even a few haughty elite in the government or the media should define press responsibility. If the press is to be princely, using its own editorial self-determination, it must constantly combat outside efforts to weaken it.

JM: But what if press freedom does, in fact, turn into irresponsible freedom--or license?

NM: "License" is a word used by freedom's cowards. Your license or bad use of freedom may very well be my positive or responsible use of freedom. A right to have press freedom gives one a license to use press freedom; there is no need for the negative term "license." A journalist should either be *for* press freedom or against it. Too many of your journalists talk "freedom" but will find ways to justify social conformity whenever possible.

JM: Is this not true with almost everybody?

NM: Perhaps. But a government official, for instance, does not have the traditional and constitutional freedom guarantees that a journalist has. There is no reason (other than cowardice or an unrealistic concern with conventional ethics) for a journalist not to feel secure in using freedom.

JM: But in so using freedom, can't a journalist go too far and become unethical?

NM: We're going to talk about ethics later this week, so I won't get into that now. I'll just say that a journalist has the right to "go too far" (in your estimation) as he uses his freedom.

JM: So, in conclusion, Nick, do you have any last words about press freedom?

NM: In reality press freedom is press power exercised by strong-willed persons. It is freedom that may be directed by the leadership of the press, but may not be interfered with by outsides forces. Freedom is subsumed by power, and is nothing but a myth aside from power. The generally powerless journalists have no freedom of any consequence. The editors and publishers and their counterparts in journalism have the power, and thus the freedom. That's about it.

JM: And that's about it for this session today. Thank you for your candor. Good day, Nick. We'll talk more very soon.

Chapter 7

Responsibility

[August 8, 1520]

JM: Now, this morning, Nick, we should speak of press responsibility. In my country we are accustomed to think of it along with press freedom and we discussed that subject yesterday. I am interested in what you say about responsibility. Why don't you just launch into some introductory remarks on this subject?

NM: Sure. Definitions abound for "responsibility," as you know. My ideas may be somewhat different from the core definition found among journalists of your country. Mine is quite pragmatic, as you might guess. It is based on success in accomplishing goals. A journalist is responsible when he achieves what he has set out to do. And even if he fails, he is *responsible for* this failure. This points out the semantic difficulty with the word. A TV station or a newspaper is successful when it is successful in getting a story. Therefore, for me, the media are responsible. If the media do not provide a good story for the public, then they are acting irresponsibly. There are many other ways of looking at "responsibility," but basically this is mine.

JM: But is not "responsibility" related to ethics--following the moral tenets of the society--and not to your idea of pragmatic responsibility?

NM: Here we go again--trying to equate ethics with the work of journalists and their objligation to provide a product to the public. One of your own journalists, Bob Sherrill, I believe you said, has put it well when he says that if a journalist has a good feeling of satisfaction with results, he is inclined to pass over ethical questions entirely. His responsibility is to get the story, and whatever works in getting the story, Sherrill says, he is for it. Now that is what I have meant by *public* morality--something quite different from one's *private* or personal morality. Sherrill has the proper attitude toward responsibility. Getting all tied up in traditional ethical considerations will most likely lead to failure--and then the public is penalized. Where is the press responsibility then?

JM: Who should set the norms for responsible journalism in a society?

NM: The Princes of the Press or the Princely Press itself should set the norms, of course. As I said yesterday, press freedom belongs to the press and with this freedom comes the right to define responsibility. Freedom implies press-determination of its social responsibility.

JM: But don't the journalists--the Princes of the Press, as you call them-- have to consider the *people* or the society in their determination of responsible journalism?

NM: Naturally.   But it should be a *pragmatic* and *egocentric* consideration. Of course the press needs the people; it needs an audience, subscribers, viewers. Therefore, the press must cater to the whims and wishes of the audience to a considerable extent. This is good pragmatics. Give them what they want--or enough of what they want to hook them. By doing this, the press is providing a desired service which, of course, is to the advantage of the press. Then the press can also give the people what the press wants them to have.

JM: But what if the general taste of the public is low and the people mainly want superficial news and entertainment trash? Don't journalists have a responsibility to set their own standards for the public--to give them not what they want but what they ought to have? Don't the people need to be lifted up, not talked down to by the press?

NM: Those are interesting questions. *I* am often thought of as being arrogant, but the thrust of those questions indicates a terribly arrogant attitude by the journalist. Here I have been trying to inject a little democratic ideology into my answer by letting the people largely determine what they want from the press--and here you are indicating an autocratic, elitist, stance by the press. Careful! Our roles must not become reversed. Ha!

JM: But, Nick, I see your "concern" for the people's wants as predicated on the press's own need to succeed, not on a sincere desire to help people. Is not your motive for journalistic utilitarianism only a pretense--a kind of "cover" for your basic success-oriented pragmatism?

NM: Motive, motive. Your insinuations are too full of Kant. No pun intended. But, listen: what difference does it really make that I have an egocentric motivation for my action? Helping myself and helping others are not necessarily mutually exclusive concepts, even under traditional moral reasoning. In order to profit, to succeed, I will use others if need be. By "using others" in this case, I mean giving them enough of what they want so that they will continue giving me their support. Many of your journalistic media realize the validity of this principle. Others, however, are pulled so constantly by altruistic forces--without the internal core of self-aggrandizement--that they are in danger of collapse.

JM: Are you against altruism completely?

NM: Of course not. A journalist, for instance, should be altruistic when it pays to be. Think of others, but first think of self. Or, said perhaps a better way, *think of others for the sake of self.*

JM: Isn't that a very cynical view of personal responsibility?

NM: Not at all. It is a very practical view. It puts responsibility where it should be. Responsibility, as you Americans might say, begins at home. I owe responsibility first to myself, then to others. Unless, of course, I need to be responsible to others first in order to bring a greater reward to myself. That's the nature of pragmatics, and the core of my concept of journalistic responsibility.

JM: How do you feel about the great emphasis given these days in my country to press responsibility?

NM: All the talk about "responsible journalism" heard everywhere in your country is simply rhetoric--largely used for self-gratification or for public relations purposes by the mass media. But the mere use of the term "responsible" means little or nothing. As I see it, there are really four ways responsibility in journalism can be used. Do you want me to go into them?

JM: Yes, by all means.

NM: First, there is responsibility *to the majority norm*. Second, there is responsibility *to the minority norm*. Third, there is responsibility to *some kind of general moral or ethical norm*. And, fourth, there is *my kind* of responsibility: *to pragmatic reality or to success*

JM: Please be more specific. I'm afraid I don't understand.

NM: What do I mean by these media responsibility norms? Well, if I am a journalist I can be responsible to the main groundswell position of my society. And this is not necessarily moral in the usual sense of the term. For example, if a majority of a state's people believe that capitalism is the best system, then as a journalist I am responsible if I support capitalism and do not try to discredit it or bring it down. If I do not support this "majority position," I can be considered irresponsible. Next, I can be responsible in the sense of defending or supporting a *minority* position. If I go along with the majority and fail to support the minority, then I can be considered irresponsible--at least by the minority. These two concepts are rather clear-cut; a journalist isolates the object of responsibility and thereby knows (in a pragmatic way) how responsible his actions are. The third position is more difficult, and it is what makes the concept of "responsibility" in journalism so nebulous, if not meaningless. This is the *moral view* of responsibility, whereby the journalist tries to give some kind of non-pragmatic, amorphous, philosophical, or religious meaning to "responsibility." Here the journalist is not responsible to some segment of society; rather he is trying to be responsible to some philosophical principle that is detached from the real world and the way things really work. This third position causes difficulty. It is why one man's responsible journalism is so often another's irresponsible action. For there is no *universal absolute morality*. It is interesting to note that while one newspaper will print a person's name, another will not; one magazine will "invade the privacy" of a grieving parent, another will not; one TV station will show a certain picture of a murder scene, and another will not.   In these cases, which media are responsible and which ones are not? There is no solid answer to such questions.   And, then there's the fourth position--*mine*. Egocentric pragmatics. Do what is best for youself and your purpose and let the chips fall where they will--and many, of course, will fall in socially helpful places.

JM: All right, Nick. As we come to the end of our session today, let me ask, how can we know if we are being responsible?

NM: The question is meaningless. What is important really is to accomplish your purpose. In a way, this is having a sense of responsibilty to success. If I set out to get certain facts for a story and I get them, then I am responsible. If I do not, then I am irresponsible. Perhaps we could substitute the word *successful* for the word *responsible*.

JM: But doesn't that mean that one is not responsible if he or she fails in an endeavor? Is not that unfair to the journalist who means well and tries diligently to accomplish his or her objectives but does not?

NM: Looked at from conventional morality, yes. But conventional morality is not what a vibrant press system must rely on. Too often it will lead to a weak and disoriented journalism, devoid of vigor, wallowing around in relativity and indecision. The responsible journalist is one who is goal-oriented, first, and success-oriented, second.

JM: But is not your view of journalism extremely selfish or inward-leaning? Should not journalism be a social or "other-directed" activity aimed at social or national advancement?

NM: I've already gone into that to some degree earlier. What I can say is this: if that is what a certain press system or a certain publisher wants, yes. Then that is a goal which is chosen, with the concomitant responsibility being its achievement. You must remember that "selfish" motivations are not necessarily contradictory to "altruistic" actions. But I've already said that. And you may recall that your Mark Twain elaborated on that view, saying in effect that *all* actions are motivated by selfishness or egoism.

JM: Are you saying that if a publisher or editor chooses to have a policy that advances what he sees to be natural progress, he is doing it for a selfish reason? And are you saying that if he achieves his goal, he is a responsible journalist?

NM: Yes, that is what I'm saying. I've got nothing against altruism--or against egoism, for that matter. That's not what is important. What is important is having a goal and achieving it.

JM: But what if the press's goal is harmful to the public interest? Would not the achievement of such a goal be irresponsible?

NM:	I suppose so, according to conventional morality. But even so, I might ask: How does the press know, at the time it sets and achieves its goal, whether or not it will be helpful or harmful to the society?

JM:	I guess that it can't be sure ahead of time.

NM:	Then, I would say that the setting of the goal and the taking of the action to achieve it could not, even by the standards of conventional morality, be considered irresponsible.

JM:	But, as I take it, you would not consider it irresponsible *even if* the press knew at the time of action that it would possibly harm the public?

NM:	Such a question gets us into really deep water, as you Americans like to say. As I have intimated earlier, we must consider "responsibility" from at least two perspectives. First, from the point of view of the *actor* and from the point of view of the *receivers* of the action. The journalist, according to this idea, would be responsible if he takes an egocentric action that would achieve his goal. The receiver, or the person affected negatively by the action, might consider the journalist irresponsible. So you see, it depends on whose goose is baked--or, as I believe you usually put it, on whose ox is being gored.

JM:	But are you saying that there are no absolute or standard criteria for press responsibility?

NM:	I thought I had already addressed that. But let me say that you have interpreted me correctly. That is exactly what I am saying. If the term "responsibility" has any meaning at all, it means nothing more than determination to succeed. If I have a goal, and *am not* determined to succeed in its achievement, then I can truly say that I am not responsible.

JM:	But, Nick, you are redefining the term to fit your own views. Aren't you playing the little semantic game played so well by Alice in Wonderland?

NM:	I suppose you are referring to Alice's contention that people can use words any way they wish. Of course she was right, but you might remember that she was in Wonderland, not in the real world. I deal with the real world, and I am trying to use words basically the way most of the people use them. Or--I am using them in *my own way* in order to bring about my ends in the real world.

JM: But most people think of responsible journalism as that which has the public's interest at heart: journalism that is honest, forthright, truthful, and things like that.

NM: I find it strange that you know what most people think about journalistic responsibility. But let's grant that you are right. If responsible journalism is what you think it is, then I must insist that there is no responsible journalism out there in the real world?

JM: What do you mean by that?

NM: I mean that journalists do not know, at the time they do their journalism, *what* the public interest is. They simply proceed in their actions to achieve their own goals, to satisfy their own desires, to fulfill their own values, and to accomplish what they see as their journalistic ends. But in all of this, they act out of their own subjectivity, not out of some objective calculus designed to satisfy the people.

JM: But how do you come to this conclusion, Nick?

NM: Simply by common sense, and by watching people--in all walks of life--making decisions and taking actions.

JM: But can't the press act so as to please the public?

NM: Which public? After all, even your own sociologists say that there are many publics--even publics within publics. Yes, the press can satisfy some people in a public, or can possibly please a whole public now and then, but it cannot satisfy the desires of *the* public. How can journalists know what pleases *the* public? Surely you realize that there is never--or hardly ever--a consensus or unanimity of thought or opinion among large groups or publics.

JM: The press cannot please everybody, of course, but what I am asking is this: can't the press try to satisfy as many people as possible, or can't it please the *majority*?

NM: Sure, I suppose the press *can* try to please the majority in its journalism, if it could know the wishes of the majority. But I can make a case that, if this were done, it would be irresponsible, not responsible.

JM: How can you say that?

NM: Well, aren't you concerned about the desires of the *minority* or the *minorities* out there? Isn't that the conventional morality that, I suspect, you subscribe to? If the press simply tries to satisfy the majority, how would that be responsible--or fair, if you prefer--to the minority? Would not you thus be taking away their right to fair treatment? But, I'm sorry, I really should not be asking you questions like this. You are the interviewer.

JM: I won't attempt to answer those questions, for I'm sure they were simply rhetorical.

NM: Good. I really did not expect answers. I doubt if it will be profitable to pursue this much further. I guess what I am saying is that responsibility is in the eye of the beholder. And, as I behold it from the perspective of a journalist, my responsibility would be pursuing successfully a goal that I have set for myself. If that is not true, then why should one be a journalist?

JM: All right, Nick. I think I understand a little better what you think of journalistic responsibility. It doesn't seem consistent with the beliefs of most of my country's journalists, but it is probably a position with which some of them can identify.

NM: Oh, I think almost all of them can identify with my position. Some teachers of conventional ethics in journalism may not agree, but most journalists, I think, would agree with me.

JM: Well, that may be so. Thank you, Nick, for this session. I do appreciate your time. I'll see you tomorrow.

[As I left our interview and was going through the small hallway to the front door, I heard Machiavelli speak to someone in another room. I do not know just who that was, for I must say that I had not met another soul in the house. I did, however, sense that there were others there. I assumed that his wife was somewhere about, although I had never been introduced to her. Or, it could have one of his children who came to San Casciano from time to time.]

Chapter 8

Self-Aggrandizement

[August 9, 1520]

JM: Terrible day out. But your geese seem to like this rain. I understand you normally don't get much rain this time of year.

NM: Not much. Let's get to the interview. I have some work to do on a speech I'm giving in Florence the end of the month.

JM: Sure. I want to hear your ideas today on the benefits of self-promotion, egoistic development, and of self-aggrandizement in general. Related to journalism, of course, if that is possible.

NM: But I've already said about all I can about that subject. My whole philosophy of journalism revolves around the concept of enlightened self-interest, of personal aggrandizement, if you will. The journalist should be as autonomous as possible. I believe I said yesterday that journalistic responsibility has its genesis in self-determination of objectives and self-discipline in achieving these objectives.

JM: But you seem to be stressing self at the expense of others. I know how you feel about altruism, but surely you want to be respected and loved by your fellow men.

NM: What helps me often helps others. But if not, so be it.

JM: What does that "so be it" mean?

NM: It is just that. So be it. I cannot, and will not, worry about the consequences of my journalistic actions. They will probably benefit or help some, and perhaps will do damage to others. That's life, as the French are fond of saying.

JM: Pardon me for saying so, Nick, but you seem a little preoccupied, even a little hostile, in your remarks today. Is there something wrong?

NM: Some personal problems, yes. I won't recount them. Also I have a bothersome headache. Don't know why. Maybe this gloomy rainy day. My geese may like the rain, but not I.

JM: Well, I am sorry, and I know you have other work to do, so we'll make this session shorter today.

NM: Good.

JM: Let me see if I can get my planned questions into one so that can save some time. If *all* journalists think first of themselves and push their own agenda, would not this be harmful to journalism as a whole and make the entire media institutions chaotic?

NM: Sure, there would be friction. Conflict will result. And media institutions, as you call them, will reverberate with discordant voices and ideas. So what if each journalist pushes himself and his own ideas and objectives? One's will is extremely important. The journalist must have a *will* to self-development, to self-aggrandizement, and to personal achievement. The *will to power*, that is the key .

JM: But, Nick, didn't the philosopher Schopenhauer tell us that we must try to subdue, even eliminate, the *will*. It is only then, he said, that we can avoid the frustrations of the world, the constant striving, the eternal *Angst*.

NM: You're right. That mystical, weak-minded, pessimistic German did say something like that. That's to be expected of someone who forsook Western thinking for the self-denunciation concepts of the Far East. I had rather concentrate on his fellow German, Friedrich Nietzsche, and his idea of power and its basic motivation--the *will*. Now, there was a man for you: Nietzsche. Standing like a Greek god among us, he urged a repudiation of the weak, feminist characteristics of humility and altruism and recommended a transvaluation of conventional morality. Without *will*, one is nothing, he said. And, as you may know, I have suggested the same thing. Schopenhauer was an escapist from the rough and tumble of life. Nietzsche was one who said "yes" to life, injected himself into it with passion, and built his ideological and pragmatic life at the foot of the volcano.

JM: But your idea of *will to succeed* will lead to social instability, to unsettling competition, and a rather chaotic society. Is that not true?

NM: So what if each journalist pushes himself and his own ideas and objectives? Some will win out and other will founder and die. Is not this the idea of your vaunted marketplace or free-market theory? Or is it not a kind of Social Darwinism applied to media institutions? What will happen is that the tough-minded, energetic, ambitious journalists will rise to the top. Now, I see that as *good* for journalism, not harmful as you suggest.

JM: But, Nick, why is it that armies are strictly regimented, the collective and not the individual is emphasized, and there is little room for personal striving and experimentation? Is not this a sign that cooperation and a spirit of communitarianism is helpful to a smooth-running institution or society? And should not this be the case in journalism?

NM: Bad analogy. An army is one thing; journalism is quite another. Soldiers are expected to be cogs in the wheel. They strive not; neither do they toil in any autonomous way. They move at a command; they have no real agenda, no real priorities. They wait for their step-promotions, their petty salary increases, their commendations for not rocking the boat. They've no independent wills; that's why they are soldiers. Puppets--or robots, as you might call them--with minimum autonomy or desire for it. One for all, and all for one. No real self-dignity and no significant will. But, for all of this, they are useful. I've always sort of liked them--but, then, I like my geese, too.

JM: But if I may break in. How are they different from journalists?

NM: The geese?

JM: The journalists.

NM: I was about to tell you. Journalists are intellectuals, and as such, aspire to much greater independence or autonomy. Well, perhaps not very many of them are true intellectuals, but they aspire to be. They would certainly admit to self-interest, to substantial ambition, and personal will. This is why so many of them consider themselves "professionals." Professionals put great stock in *themselves* and their own abilities and ambitions. Self-aggrandizement is a basic assumption for the journalist. Most all of them take a shot at it. Most fail, however; they never really get anywhere. They just repeat some routine job over and over, year after year-- always taking orders and letting others think for them. These are much like soldiers. But, contrary to soldiers, a sizable number of journalists are ever pushing, planning, conspiring, working hard, or at least cunningly, using their strong wills to move up the ladder. They are striving for power. And they know that with this self-aggrandizement philosophy, they will gain power. And power opens doors to freedom, self-respect, dignity, prosperity, and--for the journalist especially --social impact.

JM: You sound as if you respect journalists more than you do soldiers. Is that right?

NM: Not necessarily. There are good soldiers and there are good journalists. The good soldier is obedient, dependable, organized. The good journalist is creative, strong-willed, and intelligent. Certainly there are exceptions in both camps. I'm just saying that journalists in general, because of the nature of their activities, are more individualistic and self-centered. Admittedly, this self-centeredness is not always rational, but it often is.

JM: What do you mean by *rational* self-centeredness?

NM: Your controversial woman philosopher, Ayn Rand, had much to say about that. I mean much the same as she did--except for me rational self-interest   or self-centeredness is basically that concern for self that is motivated by *success and the acquisition of power*. So I would probably substitute "pragmatic" for "rational." Whatever results from my thinking and planning is that which *works* for me, that helps me achieve my ends. This, for me, is *per se* "rational."

JM: And if your plan does not work, then it is "irrational"?

NM: Correct.

JM: Most journalists, I think, are in favor of getting ahead, of helping themselves in life, but they seem to consider an altruistic journalism very important, too. Would you deny this?

NM: Of course I would not flatly deny it. But too often most of them, the wimpish segment, let the feelings and wishes of others determine their actions. Now, don't misunderstand me: I am not against considering the feelings and desires of others. But only when such consideration can help the journalist. My short motto is this: Help others if it helps you. Be kind to others if it augments your image or helps you achieve your purposes. But do not waste valuable time on others if nothing positive for you is likely to result.

JM: You seem to be saying that a journalist should by and large shun people who cannot help him in some way. Is that right?

NM: That is right. Use them or lose them. And, I must say, that generally people get in the way of an individual's success. Chances are that they are trying to use you, too--although I believe that most people are not clever enough to use others effectively.

JM: Then you would say that most people are ethical or try to be ethical?

NM: Yes. Ethical in the conventional sense; they are *privately* ethical, but I am talking about *public* ethics--ethics that applies to an institution like journalism.

JM: But you would not purposely *injure* people to satisfy your own ends, would you?

NM: Generally, no. It usually is not necessary. Remember that I said: *use them or lose them.* I did not say: use them or *abuse* them. Just keep away from helpless, clinging, pitiful people; normally they can't help you, and usually they can make life miserable for you. Of course, sometimes it is necessary to deal with weak people, if they are obedient and reasonably energetic, but it is always a good thing not to suffer fools gladly. Or even at all. Just a minute!

[**At this point, Machiavelli sprang from his chair, rushed slightly hobbling out the front door and yelled and wildly gestured at two geese that had been honking beneath the window by which he had been sitting. The geese took half-flight and honked into the shrubs that lined the far edge of his little garden. Panting a little and with raindrops glistening on his face, Machiavelli returned to his chair and frowned impatiently at me. I got the message.**]

JM: Sorry about that interruption, Nick. I guess you have, at times, trouble even suffering foolish geese gladly. Although I would like to talk more   about using people, I will   stop here and let you get about your business. Thank you for your time, and I hope you are feeling much better tomorrow when we talk about journalism and its relationship to government or the state.

Chapter 9

The State

[August 10, 1520]

NM: *Buon giorno. Buon giorno.* Come in. I'm in a much better mood today. Rain gone. Headache gone. Great day.

JM: I'm glad, Nick. For today we are to talk about a very important and interesting topic: the relationship of the state to the press.

NM: Good. I guess you know that I am very much a "statist," but I do have some ideas about the press's importance and how the two institutions should relate.

JM: Generally in my country we look at the state and the press as adversaries. I would think this would be in line with your thinking . . .

NM: Yes. The Princely State and the Princely Press. That's the way I look at it. Princes may be princes but they have power mainly in their own worlds. Ultimately, of course, I believe the state should have the power, but really it is always a contentious relationship--at least this is the case in a relatively free system such as yours.

JM: Could you clarify that?

NM: Well, journalism and government are bound to be adversaries--even when government has a so-called "iron control" over journalism. There is always a power potential for the press and trouble may erupt at any time. As I have said elsewhere, the state must do what is necessary to persist and to accomplish its objectives. Likewise, the press. So these two power institutions naturally collide and each must fight vigorously to remain viable.

JM: In the daily struggle between press and state, who would you say has the advantage?

NM: Short-term, the press. It has the first word and the last word. It can make or break many politicians if it is canny. It often does not do this because of its perceived moral role in society and its sense of "fair play." But it can bring down almost any government leader if it really sets out to do it. In fact, it can bring down *a* government--maybe not *the* state, but a specific set of people making up a government.

JM: How should the state and journalist coexist?

NM: I'm not sure what you mean by that, but I'll try to say something about press-state relationships. As I have said, they are both power institutions, seeing themselves as socially indispensable. This means that ultimately they will clash. Friction is natural between state and press, however Marxist philosophers (and your communitarians) have tried to deny it. Sooner or later the clash will come, often in small ways, but it will come.

JM: The adversarial relationship between government and journalism is said to be a good thing in my country--or at least it *was* said until about the close of the century. What you are saying is consistent with that belief, is it not?

NM: Yes, I suppose I am reinforcing that belief to some degree. But you may mean something different. I'm saying that friction is *natural* between press and state; in your country you are saying that is is *socially useful* and so it is therefore "good."

JM: But don't you think it is a socially useful--a good--thing?

NM: Not necessarily. At times it may be; at others, no. On many occasions the press would be more sensible to cooperate with government-- especially if it could achieve a certain short-term or long-term goal. And vice versa. Governments must learn to use the press. And the press must learn to use the government. In a sense it is princes using each other--ha! Of course, I know that in your country they do this to some extent--but too often "principles" of traditional morality seem to get in the way of pragmatism.

JM: What do you mean by principles of traditional morality getting in the way?

NM: It is related to what I was talking about earlier about the press's erroneous idea about moral responsibility. At the root of this idea are "principles" to which the press pays allegiance. Abiding by such principles--for example, "playing by the rules" or "being fair"--will keep the press from besting or "using" the government. The only correct principle is the *principle of pragmatism,* and the press had best recognize it. Otherwise the state will generally use the press for its own purposes and will, in time, tend to dominate it.

JM: Why do governments all seem so afraid of the press and desire to use it or to dominate it?

NM: Because the state recognizes sources of power when it sees them. The press is obviously a potent power, and when it determines to use this power with resolve and craftiness, it is the one social institution that can prove to be a worthy opponent of the state. Governments, therefore, are suspicious of the press--actually *afraid* of the press. And what you fear you tend to try to dominate or eliminate. Both press and state are extremely powerful leviathans, to use Hobbes' term, and when they lock in battle, all of society shakes.

JM: That may be true, but in my country this seems never to happen. Both press and state are reluctant to take on the other frontally. They both politely waltz around direct controntation, and both use their power sparingly. Why is this?

NM: Because both state and press are not really aware of the immense power they have. Or, then, maybe they *are* to some degree, and this keeps them from confrontations where either or both may lose some of this power. Each pulls its punches so as not to endanger its power position. Some segments of each institution, of course, are sometimes not so inhibited, to be sure, and instances of pure warfare do break out from time to time. "No holds barred" tactics are to be found between state and press, but not often. And, also, each institution has some kind of idea that it must be "fair" and abide by unwritten rules of good sportsmanship.

JM: Why do you think each side is reluctant to be more forceful? The idea of an adversarial relationship is a foundational belief in our culture.

NM: I have already said their sense of fairness militates against it. Also it is that they are not strong-willed enough. They do not want to win, to succeed, to dominate enough. Both sides are too concerned about playing by the *private* rules of morality and not overstepping normal expectations.

JM: But don't you think they *should* play by the rules?

NM: Which rules? Whose rules? There are no rules for a public institution but the *ad hoc* rules of winning, of succeeding, of besting the opponent. The good journalist, like the good government person, makes up the rules as he goes along--rules that are tailored to the particular situation. None of this Kantian formalism and "duty-bound" moralism here: just pure Nietzschean *will to power*.

JM: But isn't it socially useful for an adversarial relationship to exist where no side actually "wins"?

NM: Again, *maybe*. But how can you say that it is socially useful for government to be thwarted at every turn by an obstinate press--especially in times of national crisis or during wartime? I know what you Americans say about the press "checking the excesses of government" and all. That may be true, but it is not necessarily beneficial. Often the government must be *excessive*--and certainly *secretive*--in order to achieve its purposes. When these "excesses" are frustrated by the press, government policy may be weakened or even scrapped. And who is to say that the press knows better than the government what should be done?

JM: But, Nick, you sound as if you are in favor of censorship and government secrecy.

NM: You are right. I am. The viability and purposes of the state take precedence over the whims and purposes of the press. Friction is all right, but when all is said and done the state must triumph. The state is ultimately more important than the press.

JM: What roles do you assign to press and state?

NM: I see the press in its proper role as a power-unit in society that should strive to maintain its power and to accomplish its goals.   But I see government as the overriding power-unit whose main duty is to keep its power, expand it, and to keep the society--including the press--viable.

JM: But will not these similar purposes collide? How will such a collision be reconciled?

NM: As I have said, my belief is that government is paramount. More power is situated there than anywhere else, and it is only the irresponsible government that permits this power to erode. The government must make sure that the press does not countermand its purposes--at least its important ones. A sensible government, of course, will give the press a few small victories now and then--just as I would throw a few bones to my neighbor's dog to keep him quiet and friendly. But the government should never give in to the press. Occasionally the state will take a tactical step back in regard to the press, but for every retro-step it will take two steps forward. This, by the way, is a principle Stalin and Mao and other Marxists of the 20th century adapted from my ideas.

JM: But what about the press? What is its obligation?

NM: Likewise the press must have its objectives, its priorities, and it should use every means to achieve them. Intelligent journalists will realize that often their objectives and those of government are not contradictory; here they should cooperate. But when the press has goals that are not consistent with those of government, then the press should use any weapon in its princely arsenal to achieve its goals. The press is so diverse, so scattered, so pluralistic that it is difficult for the state to control. Its great strength lies in its diversity--both in media units and in its journalistic personalities. What can a government really do about a very diverse press? Very little without resorting to the most stringent use of power. The state, of course, will try to limit this press diversity, but the press must constantly fight against this. Diversity, you must remember, is the press's greatest defense against an intrusive state.

JM: So, Nick, what will be the outcome of this relationship? Will one conquer the other?

NM: Who really knows the answer to that question? In all modesty, even

I do not know. It may be that the press will disappear, largely from its own internal weakness and timidity. And perhaps it is a fluid relationship that will persist so long as governments themselves exist. Societies need communication--but not necessarily the press. Governments need channels of communication in order to reach the people, but there may well be better ones developing over time than the press. Who will win? Who knows? Perhaps both the press and the state are "winners" *and* "losers." Both obviously have to compromise now and then in their adversarial roles; and these compromises spell a certain loss and a certain victory. It's not a clear-cut war; it's more like family feuding or bickering. The family stays together because various parties need one another, but they are constantly embroiled in friction.

JM: But why can't government do without the press? Why can't the state simply use its own communication channels?

NM: Of course, this is possible. Your long-time neighbor Fidel Castro was very good at that. But there is always the danger that people won't have faith in government-controlled media. The state, if it wants to prosper, needs credibility and this does not come from having its own mass media.

JM: Thomas Jefferson, one of our greatest presidents and statesmen, once said that he would prefer the press to government if he had to choose. What do you think about that statement?

NM: I think it is ridiculous. That is, if Jefferson really said it, or meant it. How can you have a press without a government in the first place? Certainly Jefferson was joking. And if he were simply making the point that he thought journalism was more important than government, he couldn't have meant that either. Government is essential. The press is important but peripheral. Jefferson, who was definitely an intelligent person, surely knew that. One thing I do recall: the American *povernment* certainly treated Jefferson better than did the American press.

JM: You say the press is peripheral, but you also imply that the press is "princely," that is, powerful and essential. Are these ideas not contradictory?

NM: Not at all. I have said that the state is essential; I have never said that the press was essential. The state is paramount, and in your world the head of the state is really more of a king than a prince as I have used the term. The press operates alongside the state, supports to a great extent the state, and has its good share of power in the society. Therefore, the press is indeed "princely," but it must take second place to the state in which it exists. The press, nevertheless, must assume its princely status and, within its own inter-relationship with the people and the state, exercise as much power as possible and determine that its strength will not be dissipated by "do-gooders" in the public. It must not permit itself to be weakened by those in the public who call for a more democratic, community-minded and socially responsible media system.

JM: But your strong state will inevitably drain power from the press. Is that not right? And one more question: Does not the press assume too much power, especially in nations where state officials are elected and the press leadership is self-imposed?

NM: Good questions. Of course the state limits press power, and that's as it should be. But the press should fight constantly against state encroachment on its power. And certainly a strong national leader must keep even the most powerful press in check. And, as to your last question: The press may well assume too much power. But it is quite natural that it do so. As I have said, power is the name of the game, and if the press is not constantly gaining power, it is losing it.

JM: But, Nick, doesn't our First Amendment guarantee of press freedom preclude the state from dominating the press?

NM: Not at all. Your Founding Fathers, however much they were creatures of the Enlightenment and valued freedom, were not fools. You should note that the First Amendment says that *Congress* shall not pass laws to abridge press freedom. It says nothing about the Executive and Judicial branches of government. So your president can curb press freedom constitutionally, and so can the Supreme Court. So the state, if it is not afraid to go against public opinion at times, *can indeed* curb or restrict press freedom.

JM: That's interesting, but I doubt if many of our journalists would buy what you have just said. Nevertheless, I feel that in my country it is not the state that is draining the press of power. In large part it seems to be the press itself as it becomes ever more sensitive to public criticism. It is becoming very cautious and listens increasingly to its lawyers.

NM: Surely that does seem to be what is happening in your country. An ever more timid press, hiding behind lawyers , audience surveys and focus groups of citizens. As I have contended, timidity leads to loss of power, and loss of power for journalism means death.

JM: Would the death of journalism be catastropic for society?

NM: Not necessarily. Information would still get around; in fact your increasing reliance on computers, the Internet, and the World Wide Web and other alternative means of communication makes the press something of an anachronism. Soon you will be able to do without the "press" as you have known it; instead more and more people will see themselves as a type of journalist. The whole concept of journalism will be changing in the 21st century and the press as such will probably consist of a few fact-collecting agencies feeding into a giant computer in the sky. And, then, that is where the power will be--in the hands of the elite group that will serve as the "super-gatekeepers" of information.

JM: But let's get back to today, Nick, at least to *my* today. As we conclude this interview, let me ask you what would be your advice for a proper press-government relationship?

NM: I would say that each should try to gain as much power as possible and keep it. Beyond that, each should have definite goals, purposes-- strategies, if you will--and should skillfully make use of every tactic at its disposal to achieve these purposes. If such purposes prove to be in conflict from time to time, as certainly they will, then so be it.

JM: Do you mean that you would simply let them fight it out? Should not there be harmony between the press and the state?

NM: Sure I'd let them fight it out. Both are important and should try to hold their power. But I might add in closing that I would want to see the state win ultimately--as it undoubtedly always will. Could you imagine your Mr. Jefferson paying taxes to the press and relying on it for law enforcement and protection from foreign enemies?

[With this final question, Machiavelli rose abruptly, and looking at me with a flickering smile on his lips, headed for the back of the house. I took my leave.]

Chapter 10

The People

[August 11, 1520]

JM: Good morning, Nick. Hot out today. We could use a little more of that rain we have been having.

NM: Right. I still have not figured out how to manipulate the weather. But I'm working on it.

JM: Well, Nick, today I thought we might talk about *the people* in respect to the press and the state. I know that far too often in my country, when we're discussing journalism, we tend to slight--or even omit--the people from our consideration.

NM: Just what do you mean by "the people"?

JM: The mass media consumers. The public. I guess that is what I mean.

NM: All right. You're separating the people from the people-in-the-press. Over here you have the people, and over there you have the press. Actually, although this is a false dichotomy, it is a rather realistic view of the situation. There are two main camps. And it is a dualism that is power-structured. The press has the power, easily usable power. The people, on the other hand, have very little discernible power; and what power they have, they have little inclination to use.

JM: But, Nick, the people are essential for the press's power. And if they are essential, doesn't this give them very real power?

NM: They may be essential, but they normally don't realize it. And if they do--or some of them do--what can they do about it? People are generally programmed from birth to be led, to be guided, to be ruled. Outside a particular pressure group, labor union, or political party, they are almost helpless in the face of the state, and I might add, the press.

JM: But you feel that the people are essential?

NM: Yes, but they are essential in the same way that sand is essential for the making of concrete. You can't have journalism, of course, without people to consume it. But that doesn't give the people much power--unless, of course, they have some leadership that can coordinate their actions against the press.

JM: But what about the potency of the *vox populi* that we're heard so much about? Isn't it listened to? Doesn't it get things done?

NM: The Voice of the People is little more than a timorous whine. The people chatter about this and that, but go right on doing what they're told. They are basically helpless--like children.   The press, for example, does not trust the people (or the masses) because for one, they are fickle. Oh, your *public journalism* people may talk about the importance of the people. They acknowledge publicly that the people are out there, but they are really trying to keep up their circulations by playing the old "I-love-democracy" game. The people, generally, are simply used by the press.

JM: What do you mean?

NM: As I wrote in chapter 9 of *The Prince*, it is quite common for the people to be used by the prince (or the press) to bring about desired ends. The press must tell them lies and half-truths, raise their hopes, but it must not energize them. Then, in other instances when it suits the plans of the press, the people must see the world as caving in on them. When the people wallow in despair, then the press can easily bring snippets of hope to them. In other words, the press must bring them out, resurrect them--on and on. In this way the people become totally dependent on the press.

JM: You seem to be implying that the people have very little to do with the ongoing affairs of state and press.

NM: That's right. As your popular philosopher-longshoreman, Eric Hoffer, observed so astutely, the "game of history" is played by the best and the worst of us over the great majority in the middle. Majorities generally are weak and willing to compromise easily. Minorities, cliques, and elites-- in government, big corporations, and universities--are the main players. While the majority sits silently, these minorities make the decisions and take the actions that direct the course of history.

JM: Public opinion is not important?

NM: No opinion is important unless it can be operationalized. And in the case of "public" opinion, nobody really knows what it is. Even your Walter Lippmann found himself at a loss in trying to write about it. The sum total of individual opinions or a kind of amorphous conglomeration of main clusters of these individual opinions--that, perhaps, is as close to what public opinion is as can be formulated.

JM: But is not this simply an attempt to summarize individual opinions?

NM: Of course. Actually, I don't think "public opinion" exists--except in the mind. Not in the real world. Individuals may have opinions, but groups, masses, publics, entities do not.

JM: But is not the press reliant on the people? On their opinions? On their support?

NM: Of course. But there is no need to worry. The people will support the press if the press is skillful and crafty. The people are easy to please; just give them 90 percent entertainment, five per cent biased information, and five percent straight news. That'll do it every time. People don't expect more, nor want more.

JM: You seem to think that people generally are unsophisticated and uncritical of the press's offerings. Is that right?

NM: You're right. People generally don't expect much. That's why the press can get away with giving them so little of substance. All that is necessary is to keep their minds occupied with pap and prattle--what one of your commentators has called "chewing gum for the mind." I forget just who he was, but it is an appropriate description of your media fare.

JM: But will not the people get tired of a diet of desserts and demand more substantial and serious treatment by the media?

NM: I doubt it. People are programmed from childhood, as I have said, to expect little of real value from the media. For most people it is simply too much work to think and to contemplate concepts and ideas, to see parallels, and to try to get behind the headlines to the root causes of events. I think it would probably be too much work for the journalists, too.

JM: But shouldn't the press try to change this public attitude?

NM: Not at all. The press will keep and gain power by keeping the people stupefied with trivialities. If the people really start analyzing and criticizing the activities of the press, the press will lose power. Keep the people ignorant: that should be the strategy of the press. At the least, the people should be led to know little while thinking they know much. The press seems to be going a very good job with this strategy.

JM: Why is the press so successful in keeping the people ignorant--or semi-ignorant--about the world around them?

 NM: It's not difficult for the press. Why? Because the press itself is not very sophisticated. Its practitioners, in spite of their gestures toward erudition, are often less educated than the people--and the journalistic context in which they work forces them into superficial thinking. It is a case of the blind trying to lead the blind, except that the press is slightly less blind in some areas than the people. I'd say that the little "learning" that the people get from the press is a "dangerous learning," to paraphrase one of those English writers. But really, perhaps it's not too dangerous, since the people don't really want to wrestle with much learning, feeling that ignorance is for them no more than happiness.

JM: But can't the people see through the press's shallowness?

NM: Some of the people can, of course, but most have no real desire to. They are getting what they want--or what they have been indoctrinated to want. And that's good enough.

JM: Our President Lincoln said that you can't fool all of the people all of the time.

NM: He was right, of course. But you *can* fool most of the people most of the time, and some of the people all of the time. The press proves that every day.

JM: Are you critical of the press for doing this?

NM: Not really. The press is doing what is needed to exist and prosper with a minimum of effort. It works. And what works is good enough for me.

JM: You don't seem to have too much respect for democracy, do you?

NM: In our first conversation, back at the first of the month, I got into that with you. Let's not rehash that at this point. I'll just say that Plato was right and Socrates was wrong. You really can't trust the people to do anything but stupid things or to have any ideas but harmful ones. Only a few thoughtful and socially pragmatic figures rise up in a society to accomplish great things and to think great thoughts.

JM: Eric Hoffer, as you said earlier, wrote that the game of history is played by the best and worst among us over the heads of the great majority in the middle. I guess you would endorse that statement.

NM;   I would modify it somewhat to say that mainly it is played by the *worst* that stimulate the best into action. If it were not for the worst among us, the best among us would not be motivated to original thought and to purposeful action. When everything is all right and going smoothly, those who *can* do, do little. Adversity breeds action. And adversity is usually brought about by the worst people among us.

JM: You seem to be saying that we need the worst among us more than we need the best.

NM: You almost have it. It takes the worst to bring out the best in the best. I guess that's what I'm saying. The people generally are not very inspiring; they pass their dull, unimaginative lives on a low plane, hardly doing more than birds and bees. They are simple, easily deceived and prone to animal-like nastiness and instinctive rather than rational action. This nastiness often serves as a motivation for the exceptional person (the best among us) to react in crafty and creative ways in order to put the animal-like persons back in their place. Without such negative acts to motivate the creative person, there is little doubt that the "best" would stagnate into the general state of the worst among us.

JM: But are negative acts really needed?

NM: People respond more to fear than to love and kindness. Therefore the state and the press cooperate in keeping the people fearful and uncertain of the future. Just as well. The people are generally ungrateful, eager to avoid trouble, and are exceedingly selfish. But they are *passively* selfish; and that is why they cannot really gain power. The real powers in society--press and state--are selfish, too, but they are not passive. And they know they cannot trust the people. Give the people images, appearances and a little hope now and then--and they will be content. People care little for substance, for reality, for power. And since they are generally vulgar and thoughtless, they are only interested in appearances. What other people think of them is far more important than what they really are. They had rather *appear* knowledgeable and sophisticated than to really be. This principle, of course, explains the great success of "image-builders," the public relations pratitioners in your country.

JM: Then you would be opposed to public relations?

NM: Not at all. One must deal with the world as it is, not as you might want it to be. If people want trash, give them trash. If people want appearances, give them appearances. The main thing is to keep them from realizing what is happening to them. Multitudes of people want little...many want to "drop out." Just look at all the people on drugs, destroying what little motivation and brain-power they have. And others are throwing away their lives in other ways.

JM: Would you want to see the press try to turn these people around?

NM: Not really. Let the dope-heads drop out of society, sacrificing themselves to stupidity. Let the alcoholics and other types of crippled humanity disengage from society and any chance of power-acquisition. That will make it easier for the rest of us--fewer people to manipulate and fewer able to come into the ranks of power.

JM: That seems a very callous, or might I say inhuman, perspective to take.

NM: Better you should say *realistic* perspective.

JM: But, Nick, should not the press--and the state for that matter--try to salvage as many citizens as possible?   Is not that simple justice--the keeping of as many people in society as possible?

NM: Not at all. Justice better requires weeding out (or letting them weed themselves out) the non-productive, weak-willed creatures that lurk on the periphery of humanity.   I am saying that the press--or government for that matter--should not try to reform human nature. Just use it to their own ends.

JM: There are many Americans who would agree with you that the people are basically powerless.   There are periodic calls for "power to the people" or for "increased democratic involvement." But as I understand you, such calls are ineffective mainly because the people really do not want power. Am I right?

NM: You are right. People-power is an oxymoron.   Institutions have power; people crave leadership, paternalism, and security.   The state and press: now these are power-institutions.   They have power and want more. They pacify the people. That's why they persist and their power increases. And this is why the people find themselves estranged increasingly from the mechanisms that control them.   Their helplessness and conformity increase. Isolated deviant acts by individuals here and there do not contradict what I am saying.

JM: At this point I think I should ask you if you would like to say something good about the people?

NM: Just as the sheep-herder directs his sheep, the Prince (in government or in journalism) directs the people.   To any leader, the followers are essential, as I intimated earlier.   To the journalist, the readers, viewers, and listeners are essential.   They are all to be kept dependent.   And they must be led through the valleys where wolves menace them at every turn.   The press and the state must keep the people off the mountain tops. For it is here that insights come, that authenticity asserts itself, and fear often disappears in the rarified air.

JM: But why would you want to keep people fearful and unchallenged?

NM: Fear is the ultimate tool of the powerful. The carrot may be offered the people now and then, but the stick does the trick. Or, fear of the stick. The stick controls society. The carrot is more likely to make people escalate their expectations. True, carrots are needed on occasion, if for no other reason than to let people know what they *could* be getting. The fear of losing carrots is the greatest fear of all.

JM: Well, Nick, I'm somewhat puzzled by that last remark, but I'm recording it just the same. I'm not sure the psychiatrists in my country would agree with you about sticks and carrots.

NM: They would agree, I'm sure, especially if they were permitted to put my idea into their own words. Psychiatrists, whether or not they will admit it, are probably my most dedicated followers.

JM: Let's get back to the people. Many now believe that the people have a right to have their ideas and information appear in the press. Public access to the press it is called. Some say that people don't want to be free *from* the press; they want to be free to *use* the press.

NM: Oh, I know about your emphasis on the people's access to the press--about the Tornillo Case and Jerome Barron and all that "people's rights" business. That's ridiculous, of course. The idea that the people have a "right" to access the press was thought up by some sentimental proto-communitarian who didn't understand the foundational principles of capitalism.Of course, people have a right to *try* to access the press. That's it. The press has the right to keep them out; this goes with its freedom, as I have discussed earlier with you. And this is the way it will be in your country, unless there is a revolutionary change philosophically and judicially that will take away power from the press.

JM: Who will have the power in that case? Will this give it to the people?

NM: Of course not. If the press loses the power of editorial determination, it will be shifted to the judiciary. And that really means that the state increases its power. But I doubt if that will happen in your country. The courts already have more to do than they can handle; they surely can't take on the job of editing the press.

JM: But is it not really the people's press? Should not they have some say in its operations?

NM: This "people's press" business is a mystery to me. Even the people's state is far-fetched enough, but at least the people theoretically elect their main government officials. They certainly do not elect their press people.

JM: But it is said that the people, for instance, have a *right to know*. Since this is true, doesn't it imply that the people have considerable authority over the press?

NM: If it were true that they have a right to know, yes. But how can a free press, which you are supposed to have, be bound by an obligation to grant a so-called "right" of the people *to know*? A free press has the right to keep the people from knowing certain things. And, as I understand it, your press does just that: it keeps much information from the people. And this, of course, is the real pragmatic sign of its freedom. It is very difficult, maybe impossible, to gain and retain power if you cannot control information.

JM: Then, you don't believe that the people have much power *vis-à-vis* the press.

NM: Right. Nor do they have much power *vis-à-vis* the state. They are necessary cogs in the giant social machines propelled primarily by people of power.

JM: But they can grind the press machine to a halt by withholding their subscriptions and fees from the press.

NM: That is, of course, possible. But it won't happen. The press, as you Americans say, is "the only game in town." The people need the press just as much as, or maybe more than, the press needs them. They will go right on, in a sense, being slaves to the press and living in a world created by the press.

JM: Let's change course slightly at this point. Currently in my country there is much being made of what is known as "civic journalism," a kind of journalism that is trying to change journalism from what the press wants to publish to what the people want to read and hear about. This is an outgrowth of a new concern with reestablishing "the community," thereby bringing about more mutual communication, less social friction, and a more positive outlook. It is enjoying considerable support in my country, especially in the academic world, but also among some newspapers .

NM: Sounds like no more than a transitory fad to me. Of course I don't know very much about it, but I would say that what they are proposing is nothing new in American journalism. The very nature of journalism in a capitalistic society necessitates a strong consideration of what the people want, at least want enough buy newspapers.

JM: But, Nick, this is what I meant a few minutes ago when I said that the people have power. If they have the power to dictate editorial content in a newspaper, doesn't this mean that they have power?

NM: This is, indeed, power of a sort. But it is not real and lasting power. It is the power to be heard in part, but not really power to transform the journalism. This is still in the hands of the press managers. They are simply playing a little game with the people--making a few of them feel important.

JM: The new "civic" or "public" journalism is trying, it seems, to do a better job of meeting the people's needs. The journalists are injecting themselves more into the communities, sponsoring focus groups of civic leaders, doing more polling, and in general are retreating from the older, and more media-centered, stance of editorial self-determination. They feel this new "civic" journalism is more democratic and certainly more socially responsible than the traditional Enlightenment liberal philosophy that they see as corrupting society with its excesses inspired by press-egoism. Is not this a good start for getting people more involved in journalism?

NM: Well, as I said earlier, the people don't really want to have more editorial power. They see this as the job of the journalist, even though they may criticize from time to time. A few bored journalistic leaders and academics in universities, trying to feel creative and insightful, are proposing this kind of "people's journalism," but it will amount to little. At least it won't take root unless the journalistic leaders tire of their traditional power and turn over their journalism to the people, or rather to certain non-journalistic elites in the community. Publishers, editors and the like will not do this easily, and I see nothing really changing in your country's journalism. Journalists generally see themselves as "professionals" with special expertise in deciding what is news, and they will not, and should not, give up thiis power and responsibility.

JM: But some of our journalists *seem to want* to abdicate their traditional roles as leaders. The editor of a daily in our Midwest has stressed that citizens should not be willing to leave public life to the professionals and experts; this the editor says, will in the long run kill the democratic system. Journalists, he contends, are not humble enough; they are simply one partner with all other citizens in the conversation of our culture. What we need, he believes, is a "humble journalism."

NM: This editor is having fun, I'm sure, and is getting a lot of attention with his ideas. But if he believes the institution of journalism should be humble, he is caught securely in the net of unreality. What he secretly wants is journalism's suicide. A humble leader, a humble journalist, a humble press is idiotic. It spells the death of journalism and the rise of a kind of democratic anarchy to replace it. What people like your Midwestern editor don't seem to realize is that some power-center will prevail in journalism and if it not composed of journalists, then it will find its strength somewhere else, quite likely in corporate power, or in the judiciary, or in a strong government executive.

JM: Please respond to this, Nick, if you will. In 1997 a leading American daily got deeply into the "civic journalism" on the advice of two media advisers, and a new editor who was a devotee of "civic" journalism, was appointed. This new editor wrote, in a section devoted to explaining the paper's new stance, a letter to the people promising to help them "shape the future by providing news, information and provocative opinion" that would help them "contribute to and convey the community's conversation."

NM: The publisher of the newspaper must be grasping at straws, as you say. He talks about providing "news, information and provocative opinion." Ha. Has not the newspaper *always* given the people this? What's new? And this business about "conveying the community's conversation." That's rich! If the community is already having a "conversation," why would it be necessary for the newspaper to "convey" it?

JM: What's new about this, Nick, may be this. In the same issue of the paper, the new reformers wrote that the paper in "recent years" had been a frequent target of attack as "being aloof, detached, unengaged in the nitty-gritty of its own community." The two advisers further stated that what was needed was the new "public" or "civic" journalism that "respects and empowers the citizen reader." And they further predicted a rejuvenated paper "informing and enlarging public debate on the tough choices for the future." Now, Nick, what is your opinion on this perspective?

NM: Sounds good. Especially that part about empowering "the citizen reader." But it is all mere rhetoric, nothing but verbal ploys to justify an action of the publisher. And, believe me, I know something about rhetoric. Listen to those words again carefully and you will detect their shallowness and meaninglessness. If your "civic" journalism advocates prevail, you will find that journalists will become mere functionaries, little more than secretaries, collecting news from social groups that have their own axes to grind.

JM: You sound a little like another writer and journalist of my day, James Fallows, who is concerned about the question of where news and editorial decision are made. He writes: "Are they made in the newsrooms or at the town hall meeting . . . where the editor sups with the civic coalition?"

NM: Fallows is right to be concerned. A princely press should not permit editorial decisions to be made outside the newsroom. If this is done, the power of the press is gone, and journalists are turned into politicians or mere functionaries undeserving of self-respect or public admiration. They would be "humble" no doubt, but humility in journalism is unbecoming in a craft with such a courageous and powerful tradition.

JM: But our surveys show that journalists evoke little or no public admiration at present.

NM: Maybe not. That is probably due to the fact that their power is already beginning to wane and they are giving off vibrations of weakness. People are not going to trust a press that does not trust itself. The public journalism about which you speak is just another stepping stone to the disappearance of journalism, at least a bold, self-assured journalism that might be called "princely."

JM: Well, Nick, I think it's time to stop for today. In conclusion, would you say that in the big picture of what is going on in my country and in others that the people are relatively unimportant so far as power is concerned?

NM: In the everyday world, yes. Of course, ultimately the people *are* powerful, but only if they reach the limits of their patience, and have strong-willed leaders who will lead them into a revolutionary stage where the old power structure is destroyed.

JM: Then that is real potential power.

NM: You're right. But it seldom ever happens. And when it does, the people have only that brief moment of power.

JM: What do you mean?

NM: Well, once the old power structure is destroyed, a new one simply takes its place. The new state and the new press that assumes power continue the old practice of leading, guiding, manipulating, and propagandizing the people.

JM: On that, Nick, I think we will stop. You mention propagandizing the people, and that will be a topic we shall discuss later. Thank you, and I'll see you in the morning.

Chapter 11

Objectivity

[August 12, 1520]

JM: This morning, Nick, why don't we get to another subject that seems to fascinate journalists in my country: the concept of *objectivity* in reporting.

NM: But that's a little outside my special interest and expertise.

JM: I realize that, but I'm sure you have something worthwhile to say about it. After all, you're a very well-known historian and historians are as concerned about objectivity as are journalists.

NM: Right. It *is indeed* a fascinating concept.

JM: All right, then, let me get right to the subject by asking you if you think objectivity in journalism, or in history, is possible?

NM: It is nothing but a myth. But I suppose it is to some people a useful myth. No journalist or historian can really be objective in a report. We are all subjective creatures and all we can do is to strain reality or the objective world and happenings in it through our personal mental and perceptual strainers.

JM: What do you mean by "perceptual strainers"?

NM: Our senses. Our individualized interpretive mechanisms, as your sociologists might say. Plus, of course, our analytical and reasoning potential: our minds or our brains.

JM: And these cannot permit us to project objective reality through our journalism?

NM: They, of course, can help us strive to get close to the objective world. But they cannot permit us to convey anything objectively. You can talk all day about that black and white goose out there by the tree, but you can never report the "reality"--or the objectivity--of that goose. You are simply communicating *your limited perception* of certain outward manifestations of that goose, certainly not an objective report.

JM: You mentioned a few minutes ago that objectivity was a myth, but it is was a useful one. What did you mean by that?

NM: Well, for the journalist who is a conscientious reporter, the concept of objectivity is useful in that it is a kind of ideal out there to strive for. It is a worthy aim, although it can never be reached. Talking with my fellow historians, I often speak of the "objective of objectivity." A myth, yes, but a worthy objective for the truly serious reporter or historian. Few there are who really try to reach it, but the myth is there to spur the authentic reporters on.

JM: Why do you say that there are few who try to be objective?

NM: I say it because I have observed that it is true. Most historians--and most journalists of your day--have axes to grind. They have theories to support, programs to execute, values to project, stereotypes to create and perpetuate, political stands to take, and social and religious tenets to push. And, of course, these value-orientations propel the journalist toward ideological reportage. The journalist thus ceases being a *reporter* and becomes a polemicist; the garb of objectivity is cast away and a cloak of subjectivity is donned--often without his even realizing it. And, of course, this tendency toward "taking sides" and defending values makes it doubly hard for the journalist to be serious about objectivity.

JM: What do you mean by making it "doubly hard" for the journalist to be objective?

NM: Well, in the first place, the journalist cannot really get at reality because most of it is unavailable to human perception. As your Alfred

Korzybski said often, you can't say everything about anything. You can't even know everything about anything: if you could, then maybe you could report something objectively. But you can't "get at" the objectivity of anything. Objects are objective, but not reports of them. For instance, the tree out there is objective. You as a reporter are not objective as you try to describe it. You are subjective. That's what I meant by "doubly hard." First, reporters are opinionated, polemical, judgmental, and value-oriented by nature, as I said earlier. And secondly, they are--as I have just said-- incompetent to reach or to "get at" all of anything. Therefore, because of these two basic reasons, they are locked into a world of subjectivity.

JM: So they are destined to fail as objective reporters?

NM: Of course. They report their own subjectivity, not the objectivity of an *other*. What we get when we read a news story is a brief profile of the writer's value-system spliced together with bits and pieces of fact. This subjective *story* is part fictional, part factual, part perceptual, and part personal bias. It is hardly objective.

JM: Does this mean you are critical of reporters?

NM: Not necessarily. It simply means that they are all helpless in the face of the impossibility to reach objectivity. As Kant was fond of saying, *the thing in itself* cannot be known; only our perceptions of it can be known or described. So really, we might say that the reporter's job is no more than reflecting parts of the objective world subjectively. Some journalists--and I might add, historians--do a better job of this than others. But all are subjective in their stories.

JM: How can one reporter do a better job than another in this respect?

NM: By making his subjective report more readable, more focused, more coherent, and more memorable than the report of the other journalist. And, of course, by including more factual information of pertinence to the story. Some stories, unfortunately, are shallow or empty, while others are deeper and fuller. The deeper and fuller story is better, of course, but both fall short of being objective.

JM: As a historian, would you say that you have the same objectivity problems as the journalist?

NM: Obviously. My advantage is that I can be *fuller and deeper* in my stories than can the journalist. He must collect information and write it much faster than the historian. But in all other respects they are the same. I like to define a historian as simply "a leisurely journalist." Many of my colleagues don't think that is very funny, but it seems to me that it is a good definition.

JM: But, Nick, while I can't argue with what you have said, in my country journalists often consider themselves objective reporters. But they don't seem to mean what you mean when you use the term "objective." They appear to mean that are *factual and accurate.* Some may even mean more than that--that they are *thorough.* And others look on objectivity as an *attitude toward reporting.* Don't these journalists have a point?

NM: They have a point, but it is not a very good one. Sure, you can define "objective reporting" in a way that enables you to do it. And, if they want to consider themselves thereby objective, so be it. Nothing, however, has really changed. They are still subjective, and their stories are still biased. Their facts are highly selective; gaps are everywhere to be found; personal values impinge on the fact-selection, emphasis of parts of the story, and on the sources quoted.

JM: But my country's largest professional organization, the Society of Professional Journalists, believes that objective reporting can be done, and they say in their Ethics Code that they "honor those who do it."

NM: They are just indulging in rhetoric. Or they are simply joking. Surely a "professional" organization of journalists would know better.

JM: But would not journalism be severely damaged if objectivity were looked at in the way you see it? Would not journalists despair in their attempts to be good reporters? And, would not readers of the stories lose faith in the press as an instrument of information?

NM: Let me answer your several questions in order. No, journalism would not be severely damaged by adapting my view of objectivity. Nothing would change. Stories would still be written as they are now. And as to journalists despairing if they realize that they cannot be objective reporters, that's a laugh. For even if they use another definition than mine, they know that their stories are not perfect, that they are little more than superficial snippets of what really happened. If they are not already in despair, I doubt if what I say about objectivity will affect them very much. And, as to your last question...what was it? Something about people having less trust in the press if they thought stories were not objective. Well, as I understand it from recent polls in your country, people don't have very much faith in the press now. Press credibility is not very high. What I think bothers many people-- serious ones, that is--about the press is that it is pretentious about its objectivity.

JM: What do you mean by that?

NM: I mean that thoughtful people see the press as arrogant in its determination of *what* people will receive as news. And people feel that the press is arrogant in its privileged status and uncompromising in its self-righteousness. They see the press as saying, in effect, "What we say in the matter is the truth." This is what I mean by being pretentious about objectivity.

JM: Regardless of how you define objectivity, is not the important consideration this: what the press gives the people as news might as well be "objective" since it is all that the people will get?

NM: You are amazingly astute. The world is essentially what the press presents as the world. Important events are what the press calls important events. Heroes and celebrities are those so tapped by the press.

JM: If the world's events are different from the way they are presented by the press, we never really know it. That's what you are saying?

NM: The "if" that begins your question is needless. The world's events *are* different from the press's version of them. But you are right that generally we never know that these events are different. So really the world we know is the world created by the press. In the beginning of each day, the press starts creating the world anew. It is a pseudo-world of selected temporal events thrust into public consciousness by the creative press.

JM: But, Nick, what you are saying is ominous. The press is extremely powerful since it creates or shapes the world we take seriously every day. Are we not prisoners in a sense of a world which is constantly created by an institution over which we have little or no control?

NM: Now, you are beginning to see the situation from my viewpoint: Power. You are right about the press's potency in shaping public concerns, considerations, and values. God, it is said by the Church, created the world and everything that's in it in six days. But the press continues *every day* to destroy the old and create the new world and everything that's in it. Indeed, increasing numbers of people live in the press's world. Only those without a press of some kind live in a real or authentic world, but that world is, for them, extremely small and limiting.

JM: Would you expand on that?

NM: Well, in your so-called Third World countries, for instance, the press's world is not very important. Where the press is weak or absent, the people live in the "real" world. They determine for themselves what to be concerned about, what to talk about, what to consider important. They are not told constantly what to think, what to think about, and what they need to possess. In that sense they are freer than you are. *They are free from the press.*

JM: What you seem to be saying is that the more primitive a people are, the more directly they confront the real or objective world and the less they need to be dependent on the press to give them a "pseudo-world" in which to live.

NM: That is correct. These people in a primitive society may not be free from some kind of government control, but they are at least free from press control. Mind you, I am not recommending primitivism. People in such societies have far more negative concerns than living in the press's pseudo-world.

JM: But you are saying, I think, that objectivity in the press is impossible and that the subjective world that is provided to the people is definitely a directing force in their lives.

NM: Surely I am saying that.

JM: Do you think this is a good thing?

NM: Yes, I do. People are not prepared to face the *real* world. It is too harsh, too potent, too unrelenting, too complex. It is a good thing that the press simplifies and structures it for them. It makes it more understandable and palatable. We talk about people *becoming civilized* as they go through the process of escaping from direct exposure to reality and entering the pseudo or indirect world constructed by the media of mass communication.

JM: But the world, we say, was created by God. If so, why should the people be shielded from it? Why should not the people be able to cope with it directly?

NM: In the beginning, says Judeo-Christian theology, the world was, indeed, created by God. But that does not mean that people can deal with it in its pure form. The people need myths, stories, prototypes, stereotypes and other simplifications in order to live without too much trauma. The press is a big factor in this simplification process--it subjectivizes reality or objectivity, as I have said, thus giving some limited shield to the direct, overpowering dimensions of reality.

JM: Journalists, then, as you see them, are necessary for the psychological health of the people?

NM: I guess you might say that, although certainly the press can also stupify people by flooding in on them vast quantities of disparate and largely negative information. But journalists simplify and censor reality, too. They screen reality for the people. Of course, in my day, the real world faced by the people is largely simplified by the people's own perceptive screening. In short, they see less, hear less, worry about less, and realize less. Their sophisticated, and very provincial, perceptive mechanisms are substitutes for the press of your day.

JM: I'm not sure I follow that completely, although I recognize the importance of screening total reality from the people. As Plato put it, what we mortals really see are the shadows on the Cave wall, and not the real world at all. And, you are saying that the journalists, in effect, are those who are somehow casting these shadows of the real world. Is that right?

NM: Right. But, of course, Plato would probably say that the so-called "real" world from which shadows are cast is not actually the real world either, but simply representations of the real world--what he might call the *ideal* world (the idea behind the world). But, let's not get into that business. I think Plato was having a bit of fun with all that idealistic claptrap.

JM: I won't follow up on that, Nick. We'll let Plato's motivations lie. But I'm glad you agree basically that his ideas do relate to this subject.

NM: Indeed I do. It is fair to say that the process of casting shadows is roughly analogous to subjectivizing reality. The journalist, for example, in selecting and simplifying a happening in the real world--or in selecting from that happening certain aspects--is participating in the process of subjectivity. He is, indeed, a shadow-caster, rather than a light-caster.

JM: Well, Nick, I think we'll stop here today, although I'd like to hear more about this "light-casting" business, but I think I know what you mean. Tomorrow we'll get into a discussion of *propaganda*, one of your favorite topics.

NM: What makes you think that I like propaganda?

JM: I read it somewhere.

NM: I'll be happy to talk with you about it, but don't believe everything you read about me. One of my tavern friends recently said that he had heard I liked French wine. Actually I don't like anything French. Anyway, I'll be happy to talk about propaganda. But that reminds me: I need to get over to the tavern. See you soon.

Chapter 12

Propaganda

[August 13, 1520]

JM: I started to ask you yesterday, Nick, if we could skip today's session. Today is the 13th of August. I've always felt that the number 13 was unlucky.

NM: The number 13 unlucky? You Americans have more superstitions than I do, and that's difficult. Dame Fortune will deal her hand and we mortals are hard-pressed to do anything about it. Even with my *virtù*, for example, with which I can offset some of *fortuna*'s dictates, I know that I am practically helpless before her. Anyway, I'm glad you came, for as you recall, I want us to finish by the middle of the month so I can do a little more preparation before I'm off to Rome to talk with Pope Clement about my history of Florence.

JM: We'll finish in time. We have only two more sessions after today.

NM   Let's get at it.

JM: Propaganda--that's the topic for today. I am interested in your thoughts about the subject as it impinges on journalism.

NM: Well, that's a very tall order--like most of these you have presented to me. I'll give you some of my ideas, but as I said in our first meeting, you must keep me on the subject. I'm prone to wandering.

JM: What I want you to deal with first is the relationship of propaganda to the press.

NM: Propaganda is essential to the press--and, I might add that I agree with the Frenchman of your day, Jacques Ellul, that the press is essential to propaganda. At least to mass propaganda.

JM: But is the press simply a conveyer of others' propaganda, as is often said in my country?

NM: Of course the press conveys propaganda. But it also originates it. Its content almost always contains propaganda, especially in complex, ideologically significant stories. I've talked about subjectivity in journalism and how the journalist's values help form the stories. This is related to propaganda.

JM: Maybe you will tell me at this point what you mean by *propaganda*.

NM: Well, I can give you a shorthand version. As you know, many hefty tomes have been written on this subject. But here briefly is the way I look at propaganda. It is an attempt to persuade. Actually the term originated with the Church in Europe--an attempt to propagate the Faith. It is a purposeful attempt to persuade, but not only to persuade--but to cause those persuaded to take a certain action. You know how important action is to me. The successful propagandist, therefore, is one who spurs people to action.

JM: Action of what kind. . .?

NM: I was going to say that what the propagandist wants is for the receiver of the message to act *according to the wishes of the propagandist*. That's the key: the propaganda must be such that the will of the journalist, or propagandist, will be the same as that of the receivers of the propaganda. In other words that I may *want* to do what you are propagandizing me to do.

JM: But you're saying that propaganda is *selfish*? At least in the sense of reflecting the desires of the propagandist?

NM: Yes

JM: But what about the actual nature of the messages of propaganda? Wouldn't that have something to do with the definition?

NM: Of course. And I've already said something about the nature of propaganda--for example, it is purposeful or intentional, it is action-oriented, and it is persuasive. What you Americans call propaganda is what I normally refer to as *rhetoric* or the art of language manipulation for the purpose of gaining support of my position.

JM: What else is it? What about *deception*?

NM: I was going to get into that. In your country the term "propaganda" has a negative connotation. It is considered bad or evil, and the reason lies with what you call "deception." The propagandist is generally thought of as a person who is not only a persuader, but a *deceptive* or dishonest one. Certainly the ideas of deviousness, deception, manipulation and other sinister characteristics are important in the average concept of propaganda.

JM: But shouldn't they be?

NM: Quite often, yes. The propagandist is trying to cause people to believe something and is using irrational or emotional appeals. He is trying to manipulate people unfairly, to pull the proverbial wool over their eyes. Often, in fact, my name is given to this type of propaganda. That's not quite fair, for I believe in basically truthful and evidential persuasion *when that will work* with a particular audience. Propaganda must be flexible; it must be pragmatic. It must be tailored to certain types of receivers. If I can be truthful, or mainly so, and persuade, that's what I will do. Certainly I don't want to take chances with a sophisticated, knowledgeable audience. But, I must say that with most audiences it is safer to be devious, skillful, and crafty with the language. There is no need to be too careful with the truth. Why? Because people really don't care, and if they do, they seldom can know enough to unmask the propagandist.

JM: But is there not propaganda which is *not* deceitful or untruthful?

NM: Of course. For instance, much Church propaganda. Those who propagandize the faith are not deceitful nor are they being untruthful--so far as they know. They are spreading their *beliefs* in a forthright, open manner. But the factor that makes this kind of communication propaganda is that it is appealing to the emotions, not the intellect. And, also, there is no *proof*, no fact-based substantiation, for the message treansmitted.

JM: Well, this type of propaganda is not relevant to the press.

NM: It may be to some extent. Often it is found in advertising. And in news stories and commentary, too. But the best example, I think, is the Church. Propaganda has always been associated with the Church--but not necessarily in a negative sense. Appeal to emotion, not intellect. Appeal to faith, not evidence. Call to some kind of action. Use of crowd-psychology-- music, ritual, rhetorical sopistication, and the like.

JM: Back to the journalist and his use of propaganda. Why should the journalist who is dedicated to the truth participate in propaganda?

NM: I doubt if the journalist is really dedicated to the truth--at least not all the time. He may tell it now and then when he has no strong feelings about a subject--or when he is not pushed for time. But I would say that generally the journalist plays games with the truth--hiding it when he wants to, or giving parts of it when he wants to. And, after all, the audience is at his mercy, not knowing anything about the real nature of the events being reported. Therefore, is it hard to believe that audience members accept the journalists' stories as unembroidered truth?

JM: I still don't understand why journalists would be propagandists.

NM: In the first place, because they are human. It is human to want to persuade, and it is also human to stretch the truth for your own ends or to bolster your own argument or position. Also the journalist is in a natural power locus--with the facilities of the press behind him--to make use of this natural inclination to persuade.

JM: But doesn't the journalist want credibility? Being a propagandist doesn't help him in this respect.

NM: The journalist wants credibility, of course. But this is not the same thing as saying that he wants to be truthful and forthright. He wants *to be believed*. But he knows that if his propaganda is good--meaning effective-- he will generally be believed. He knows the audience is helpless, having nothing but journalism to give it basic information. He also knows that, by and large, the audience is ignorant, hurried, impatient, and lazy. Thus he knows that precision, accuracy, balance, and thoroughness are not really important in order to be believable.

JM: If the audience knows that journalists are propagandistic, won't that hurt their credibility?

NM: Probably. But perhaps not very much. For the people have resigned themselves to the idea that propaganda permeates the press and pours forth from government. They know it's there, but they don't know just where. They realize that they, in order to believe something, must more or less believe everything--or believe little or nothing. They have neither the time, the knowledge, nor the deep desire to dig for the truth and to analyze all the information that flows in upon them. As I said, they are really helpless.

JM: How much information in the press would you say is propaganda?

NM: Well, let's see. First there is the self-generated propaganda of the press itself. That must account for at least ten percent of a typical newspaper or news program. Second, there is the propaganda of others--government officials, people interviewed, et al--which is woven into stories by journalists. This probably takes up fifteen percent of space and program time.

JM: All right. That is about twenty-five percent propaganda.

NM: But I was not finished. Advertising is the very best example of propaganda, and as you are aware, it takes up easily sixty percent of press space. So that would mean that the press conveys a total of eighty-five percent propaganda of its total coverage.

JM: That would leave about fifteen percent that would not be propaganda.

NM: Right. But actually I have probably been too conservative in my estimates. I believe I said that perhaps ten percent of what the journalists themselves produced was propaganda. On second thought, that's probably far too low. You've got to consider editorials, personal essays, syndicated political columns and cartoons, advice columns, biased photographs, cutlines, headlines, and the like. Actually I probably should have given the figure of twenty per cent of the total press space. And I'm thinking here, of course, of the print media. If I throw in for radio and TV such things as voice inflection, facial expressions, emphasis in talk shows and panel discussions, and the like, surely this new figure of twenty per cent would not be excessive. And...then there's the propaganda added to the newspaper (and talk shows) by audience members who write letters and call in.

JM: Then that would make the press's output of propaganda about ninety percent. That's frightening! Do you really feel that we can count on only about ten percent *non-propagandistic* content from our press?

NM: Really, in my more realistic moments I would probably say that *all* press material is propagandistic. Somebody is trying to misrepresent a case, push a program, champion a value, sell a product or candidate--or in some way get others to go in the direction the communicator thinks is best.

JM: Then, you feel that almost every kind of message is propagandistic?

NM: Yes, yes. For example, I forgot to mention all the public relations practitioners who are pouring steady streams of propaganda into the press every day. They are pushing something--providing a positive image for their sponsor. Trying to keep negative aspects away from the public whenever possible. It is hard even to estimate how much propaganda gets into the press from public relations activities. So, you see that it is difficult to escape propaganda in the press.

JM: Do you think of that as bad?

NM: Not at all. I see it as perfectly natural. The person who takes the press to task for propagandizing would do the same thing if he had the chance. It's just that the press is big and powerful and has the power to magnify its voice whereas the propagandistic individual has insignificant potency. But the principle is the same: both the individual and the press are propagandists. We do the best we can with the potential we have in spreading our ideas, opinions, and biases around.

JM: In view of what you've said, is propaganda good or bad?

JM: That kind of question again. Ha. Is the wind good or bad? Good for the sailor needing wind in his sails. Bad for the family whose house is blowing away. Propaganda is, in fact, both good *and* bad. It is good for me if I like its motivation and results, and it is bad for me if I dislike its motivation and results. I had rather talk of *effectiveness and ineffectiveness* of propaganda. If my propaganda works or does what I want it to do, then it is effective--and therefore "good" for me. If my propaganda doesn't work, is *not* successful, then it is "bad" from my perspective and can be termed *ineffective*.

JM: How can people detect propaganda?

NM :   Most of the time they cannot. The propagandist is always ahead of the people. The propagandist knows something--or is thought to know something--that the people do not know. So the propagandist, or your journalist, is seen as a kind of expert who has something that the people want. The people don't want to doubt, to question, to analyze everything they get from the press. What they want to do is to believe it. That's where the propagandist has the great advantage. And it is through propaganda that the journalist, for instance, can be very effective by being crafty, skillful, manipulative, and persistent. He knows that his half-truths, lies, distortions and biased stories will seldom be challenged.

JM: Why are not the offerings of the press analyzed and challenged more often?

NM: I have said it. People are lazy. They are basically ignorant. And they are trusting. And they have better things to do. So the propagandist knows that if his propaganda is superficial, biased, repetitious, and insistent, it will generally be effective. He won't snare all the people in his net, of course, but he can count on always getting a good catch.

JM: Propaganda, then, for you is an indispensable tool for the press.

NM: It is a natural, unavoidable tool.

JM: And you see it as a positive or helpful tool for the press?

NM: Yes. The press aspires to having an impact. It wants to have power. It wants to be respected, though not loved. It must use propaganda in order to accomplish these purposes. If its propaganda is effective, and I think most of it is, then the press will continue to have great impact on the thinking and actions of the public.

JM: But many of our scholars say that there is no scientific proof that the press affects such things as crime--or even the political thinking of our country.

NM: Well, I think their scholarship needs some rejuvenation.

JM: What do you mean?

NM: That your scholars say a lot of things. Common sense tells the average person that the press does, indeed, affect society in innumerable ways. If the scholars want to believe otherwise, so be it.   They are not particularly known for having common sense. Now, if they were true *Renaissance* men, like me, then they wouldn't say such such things..

JM: But, Nick, *you* are a scholar.

NM: I am not really a scholar. I am a historian, an observer, a skeptic, and above all--a realist and a pragmatist.

JM: I wish we had time to pursue that -- the difference between a scholar and these things you say you are. But I know that you must get to your other duties. I am afraid I have stayed too long as it is. Thank you, Nick. I'll see you again tomorrow when we talk about the relationship of ends and means-- a subject I know you are interested in.

[As I was leaving, Machiavelli grabbed a hat and followed me to the door where he picked up two bird traps. We parted ways at the nearby road.]

Chapter 13

Ends and Means

[August 14, 1520]

JM: Good morning, Nick. This is the next to last interview and I hope it goes well. It should, because the matter of ends and means is important to you, I know. You wrote about it in your works, but this morning I would like to get more of your thinking on it--especially as it relates to the press.

NM: Good. This is a fascinating subject for me. I'm always happy to discourse on it.

JM: I know you say rather directly--I believe it was in Chapter 9 of *The Prince*--that often the people have to be used for the Prince's ends. This is certainly contrary to basic morality of my country that stems mainly from one version of the Categorical Imperative of Immanuel Kant.

NM: I know. I know. Up comes old Kant again with his idea that one should never use others as means, but as ends only. Kant was pretty much of an establishment ethicist, taking his core principles from Christianity. He stressed what he thought people *should or should not do*. I, on the other hand, stress what people *do* or need to do--if they want to succeed in the real world. And in his other version of the Categorical Imperative--the one saying that we should do only those things we would be willing to see universalized--he is equally naive. That would frustrate leaders and enterprising journalists almost completely. The journalist, for example, must consider himself an *exception*. Certainly he won't wish to see his actions universalized.

JM: You always seem to believe that the objective or ends of the actor to be the significant factor in any kind of determination of proper action. Is that right?

NM: I'm not quite sure what your question means. But, I can say that the ends which the journalist has, for instance, is the major stimulus for action. The ends, in other words, determine or generate the means or tactics for achieving these ends.

JM: The journalist's ends, then, in your view justify the means?

NM: Correct.

JM: Do they justify *any* means?

NM: If the ends are considered very important--important enough to pursue them in the first place--then, yes, they should justify such means as will bring them about. Some ends, of course, are so childish and unimportant that extreme means. or what conventional or *private* morality considers unethical, are foolish and most likely unnecessary. One doesn't kill a fly with a sledge hammer. Nor do all flies need killing.

JM: We'll talk more about journalistic ethics tomorrow in our final session, so I will try to keep us away from that subject as much as possible today.

NM: Although we're talking about ends and means, and that is considered generally in your country as ethically related, I prefer to say we are really talking about *pragmatics*. So, we can say we're saving ethics for tomorrow.

JM: Very good, Nick. Say a little more about ends justifying means in journalism.

NM: Well, suppose a journalist--let's say an editor--wants to have his staff members think of him as a proponent and defender of maximum in-house journalistic freedom. But really he is not. He knows, however, that his staffers want to believe that they have such freedom and that their editor supports it. So what does this editor do?

JM: Are you asking me?

NM: Yes.

JM: Well, he can *tell* them that he is in favor of such freedom.

NM: In other words, you are saying that he can lie. You are right, of course. His ends, unimportant as many would take them to be, are pursued by misleading his staff as to his values. Lying has been justified as a way to bring about his ends. Of course, he can play other games such as to set up unimportant but overt ways of making the staffers think they have freedom--such as attending editorial meetings once a month, placing ideas in a suggestion box, and bringing complaints personally to the editor.

JM: But those are rather innocuous examples. Most journalists do such things; they are just the reasonable, the diplomatic things to do.

NM: Oh, yes. And they are the Machiavellian things to do. You're right about my examples being reasonable. I was beginning with such examples to make a point.

JM: And what is your point?

NM: That journalists, without even thinking about it, quite often use whatever means they desire to bring about their ends. The editor I referred to just wanted his staffers to believe a certain thing about him. His end, however unimportant it may seem, demanded certain means, and in this rather innocuous case, as you call it, what was demanded was that the editor mislead, give an erroneous impression.

JM: And you feel that such means were justified?

NM: Of course. If the editor had a sound reason for wanting his staffers to believe that way--and he must have had such a reason or why else would he have desired it?--then his lying was quite appropriate.

JM: Let's take the case of a reporter attempting to collect facts for a story. Is he justified to use any means to get these facts?

NM: First, we must ask what is the reporter's job, his task, his objective--his end?

JM: To report the story, of course.

NM: Then, if the facts are necessary for the story, and we must assume they are, the journalist has his answer. Use the methods or means necessary to get the facts.

JM: Even illegal means?

NM: This, of course, depends on the dedication to reporting and the courage of the reporter. The weak-willed, cowardly reporter settles for the superficial, incomplete, and gap-filled story. The dedicated reporter, on the other hand, gets the facts. That means that he uses any means necessary. He is willing to take the chance in order to be good at his job.

JM: But do not all reporters have to compromise, to give up on some facts, and even on some entire stories?

NM: They don't *have to*, but most of them do. It is not easy to be a good reporter. In fact it is the most difficult job in journalism. Why? Because it demands steadfastness, and a strong determination to accomplish a very well-defined end.

JM: And what is that?

NM: To report as accurate and complete a story as possible.

JM: But, Nick, you said yesterday, when talking about propaganda, that journalists commonly propagandize, slant their stories, and the like. This would *not* seem to suggest that their end or objective was to present an accurate and complete story.

NM: Sure, they propagandize and write bad stories, but this is not their aim. The serious reporters, as I say, will take their reporting seriously. And if they do, they will resort to any means possible to provide a good, complete story. That's all I'm saying.

JM: How far would you take this? For example, should reporters hide their identities, steal records and papers, tap phones, and bug offices to get information?

NM: Yes, as I wrote in *The Prince* about governments: if governments are to be successful and viable, they are always ready to act ruthlessly to attain their ends. I would say the same thing about journalists.

JM: But this is generally thought to be wrong or evil in my society.

NM: I know. But let me repeat what I have said in my writings. Whether an action is evil or not can only be decided in the light of what it is meant to achieve and whether it is successful in achieving it.

JM: So, the reporter considers the getting of the story as a worthy end. And then he looks at his success in getting it. If the story is worthy (in his opinion) and he has gotten it; then we can say that the reporter's actions were *not* evil?

NM: That's right.

JM: And suppose the journalist decides to use conventional ethical tactics to get the facts: what's wrong with that?

NM: Nothing. If he can get the story using traditional, conventional--or what I call *private*--morality in his newsgathering, that's fine. If they work, great. Use them. There is no use antagonizing people unnecessarily.

JM: I should leave this for tomorrow, but let me ask you this. Since you have a lot to say in your writings about *virtù*, would you not think that a journalist who follows your precepts would not be very virtuous?

NM: You have not read me well on the subject of what I call *virtù*. You use my term in one way; I'm using it to mean something quite different. From your perspective and with your normal concept of the English word *virtue*, I can see how you might feel that way. But when I talk about *virtù* in my writings, as is true with most Italian writers of the Renaissance, I am thinking about efficiency, prowess, craftiness, a sense of willpower. I am associating the term with *virtuosity* and not with the moral connotation of your word *virtue*. When the journalist achieves his end, for example, he is a virtuoso even if your countrymen would not consider him virtuous in a conventional moral sense.

JM: But at times in your writing you seem to give such a moral meaning to the word *virtù*.

NM: I have been told that. And, in fact, it is probably true that I tend to use that word and many others, rather loosely. But we all need to use the language somewhat loosely. Every good politician knows that. It allows us to deny that we say what others think we say...we have a kind of escape mechanism. At any rate, words themselves shouldn't be taken too seriously. Actions are what count.

JM: But journalists need to use language precisely, don't they?

NM: No more than politicians. Journalists use words to accomplish their purposes, and one of the purposes often is to cloud issues and hide meaning. It is wrong to think that journalists are purer, more honest, more authentic, and more linguistically precise than anyone else. We all play games with language. Words are simply what we juggle in order to take the eyes of others off our real selves. Some of us do a better job of this than others, but we all do it.

JM: I don't understand.

NM: Language is simply the fabric from which images are made. Most of us are what we say, not what we are. Although what we say is part of what we are, most of us--and this is especially true of journalists--emphasize our rhetorical selves to such an extent that our true selves are lost.

JM: What is wrong with that?

NM: Nothing is wrong with it. It's just an observation. Does everything have to be right or wrong? It seems to me that most people are not open, forthright, and authentic; they want to hide themselves from others. And a good way to do this is to develop some word patterns and linguistic configurations which tend to make *what we say* equivalent to *what we are.*

JM: What does this have to do with ends and means, Nick? You asked me to keep you on the subject.

NM: Right. I was drifting off again. But, then, this does have something to do with ends and means. For example, I want people to think of me in a certain way...I want to create an image by which I am known and thought about. And I resort to language to create this image, and although this language-image may be contrary to my real self, it in a sense becomes me in the eyes of the world. My end is to create a certain image of myself. The means is language. So if I am a "virtuoso" with language, I can indeed create for myself a pseudo-self composed largely of verbal materials.

JM: But in that case I would say that the end is a rather poor one, one that probably does not justify the means of all the language creation.

NM: I don't agree. Most people inwardly, intellectually, spiritually, socially and psychologically are pretty weak. Their *real* selves are nothing much to be proud of, so it is quite natural that they want to submerge their real selves under an image. We are in fact insulated from public exposure and ridicule by our created images. We are to a very great extent what we and others *say* we are, not what we are. At least this is true in respect to our relationships with others. So, you see, people *need* this linguistic suit of armor for protection and self-respect. And when such a need exists, the linguistic means to satisfy it also exists, however inauthentic and misleading it may be.

JM: Well, Nick, we are getting to the end of this session, so let me ask you one more question. Since it seems to me that you believe people with a strong will can make a suitable objective, or end, out of almost any desire, are you saying that any means are justified to achieve any self-rationalized end?

NM: You are rather perceptive. True, I do believe that a strong-willed person can justify almost any personal objective. That is, after all, human nature. We all do it to some extent. But the exceptional person who is cunning as a fox and strong and brave as a lion will achieve his ends to a far greater degree than will all the others. Even if the action-rationales are not very strong, the true leader will act. However, even with the strongest reasons for action, the average person will stand back timidly watching his objectives fade away.

JM: But to my question. Will any means be justified to attain any *self-rationalized* end?

NM: I must answer this way: any means *will not* be justified to attain any such end, but let me say that, in my opinion, any means *should* be used to bring about a self-appointed end. Unfortunately, or fortunately perhaps, most people cringe from using workable means. Only the true *princes* of the world, among state and press, are able to throw over the traces of conventional social norms and resort to what will work.

JM: Pragmatism then, rules the world?

NM: Pragmatism *should* rule the world, but it really doesn't. More's the pity.

JM: If then, a reporter needs some papers for his story and cannot get them legally, it is all right for him to steal them?

NM: Yes, if he is a dedicated and willful reporter.

JM: And, if he gets caught and goes to jail?

NM: Then, he goes to jail. He must be willing to take the consequences for his action. Jail is not too bad. In many ways I found it rather interesting.

JM: Interesting?

NM: We can't get into that at this point, but I'll elaborate on it later if we have a chance. Dull routine and dealing with mass stupidity: these are worse than any prison.

JM: How would you sum up the main point of our interview today?

NM: Know what you want. Get it by any means possible. Don't worry about the consequences, but if they are bad for you, accept them.

JM: Well, Nick, I appreciate your forthright and interesting remarks. I must admit, though, that there are some of your concepts that I don't quite understand. But perhaps I could never understand them.. I'll see you in the morning about 10 o'clock for our final session--on ethics. I know you have already dealt here and there with this subject, but in the last session tomorrow I hope you can be more specific in your remarks. Until tomorrow.

NM: Farewell.

Chapter 14

Ethics

[August 15, 1520]

JM: Good morning, Nick.

NM: Good morning. And it really *is* a good one. Rains and cloudy skies seem to be gone.

JM: A great day for our last session on ethics. Not your favorite subject, I know, but a good one with which to end our interviews. If you were to lay claim to being ethical, and I'm sure that you don't, what theory of conventional ethics would you subscribe to?

NM: What a strange question! I am a believer in expediency, in pragmatics, in what I have called *public ethics*, and I have given little thought to what you people in America call ethics. However I am familiar with the so-called great ethicists and with a number of their theories. I guess you could call me a *consequentialist*, one who acts with consequences in mind. However, I should stress that I am interested in how my actions will affect *me* and *my* programs and not other people and theirs. As you know, I am a pragmatist and as such care a great deal about consequences.

JM: Well, John Stuart Mill is a good example of one who thought consequences were very important. He said we must do that which will bring the greatest happiness to the greatest number. He represented what we call the teleological stance in ethics, and his particular brand of teleology was called utilitarianism.

NM: I know all of that. But I am not a consequentialist like Mill. He was an altruist, thinking of others and their happiness. As I just said, that is not the focus of my consequentialism.   I am thinking of *my* happiness and success.

JM: How do you differ, or *would* you differ, if you were a traditional or conventional ethicist?

NM: Well, I wouldn't differ too much. I would be, I guess, what you call an *ethical egoist*--or an egoistic consequentialist. In fact, there are some rather conventional philosophers who actually espouse a kind of egoistic ethics, but they normally are not as pragmatic as I am, nor would they use many of the methods I would use. But I suppose I am fairly close to some of them in their thinking.

JM: But I would think that even a pragmatic egoist like you would have some sympathetic and kind feelings for others.

NM: Of course. I do! But I usually keep them in my private life and my personal relations with family and friends. I try to keep them separated from my life objectives or my patriotic feelings. Your type of altruistic ethics, with its overtones of egalitarianism, can bring you much pain. It is hard to be loving, fair, and considerate in a basically immoral society. Someone will take advantage of your goodness very quickly.   Being moral is quite dangerous among people who are not moral.

JM: To get to the main subject of our interview: would you say that the journalist would be better off if he would spend less time trying to do the ethical thing and spend more time bringing good consequences to himself?

NM: Naturally. Journalists often harm themselves, confuse themselves, frustrate themselves, by worrying about the ethics of their actions. A concern for ethics will ruin a good journalist, will make him timid, even cowardly, and will replace firm decision with indecision. Americans, I feel, spend far too much time and effort discoursing about ethics. Now, mind you, as I said in *The Prince*, I would not say to disregard conventional morality as such. When the political situation (or the journalistic one) is stable and secure, then use conventional morality. The journalist, like the prince, must be adaptable and have what I have called "a mind ready to turn in any direction as Fortune's winds and the variety of affairs require." In other words, he does what most ethical people would think is right when he can--but, "he can and knows how to do wrong when he must."

JM: But aren't there some ethical principles to which journalists should always be dedicated?

NM: Here comes Kant again! No. Not in my opinion. Even many of your philosophers say ethics is a relative matter. They talk about situationism and the like. Your Isaiah Berlin refers to "value pluralism" and sees it as a good thing. Well, you might say that my conception of *public ethics* is part of that value pluralism. Most philosophers hate to admit it, but know intuitively that there are no real principles in ethics. Immanuel Kant said that one should never lie, for example, but anybody with common sense knows that in certain situations one will lie, and can give good moral reasons for it, too. Journalists talk much about their dedication to the truth, but we all know that they play fast and loose with it. They shape it to fit their desires; they often hide it, and they have their rationalizations for so doing when occasionally they are confronted. Dissemblers: that's what most journalists are.

JM: If you were a journalist, would you not want to be thought of as ethical?

NM: Now, that is another matter. Yes, of course, I would prefer to be *thought of* as ethical. Image, you recall, is very important. But image is not reality. Obviously the image of me as ethical would be generally a good thing for me; it would enhance my reputation and thus my power. And it would be part of the *persona* that is needed to bring favorable consequences to me and my programs. If the people generally have a concept of "being ethical" that they respect, then the wise journalist will identify himself with that concept.

JM: In other words, you would try to make others *think* you are ethical even if you are not?

NM: Right. After all, isn't that what most all people do?

JM: I like to think that I am not *that* cynical.

NM: That's not cynicism; that's reality.

JM: It is hard to talk with you about ethics since you really do not consider the subject of much importance. Would your actions be significantly different from those of a person who tried hard to be ethical?

NM: In some ways, of course, they would. But in many ways we would undoubtedly act similarly.   As I told you earlier, if I can accomplish my purposes within the framework of the society, then that's what I will do. I do not alienate people unnecessarily. But, then, if I anticipate failure from abiding by general ethical norms, I will resort to pragmatism. I will bend--or ignore--the usual ethical rules or expectations. And I will resort to tactics designed to succeed, not to give me a little star on somebody's morality chart.

JM: In other words, you would be ethical when it pays, but would not be ethical when it doesn't pay?

NM: You might put it that way; however I feel that couched in those words your question evidences some hostility.

JM: Not hostility, Nick. But perhaps disagreement.

NM: I don't mind disagreement. What I am saying is that the journalist, to be successful, must on occasion set aside the generally respected ethics of his society and launch out into pragmatic waters. After all, nobody *really* knows what is right and wrong--it is only convention that makes it so. Therefore, the good journalist is one who is determined to succeed, and in order to do this he often has to determine *his own* ethics or moral convention. Quite likely he will be as ethical as the next person, although he may go against normal social expectations.

JM: But are not social expectations important?

NM: Not really, except to the weak person who wants a paternalistic environment, who wants to be guided by the values and opinions of others, who does not want to take charge and make autonomous decisions.

JM: But are all persons who want to live in a harmonious society weak?

NM: According to conventional, or better, Christian morality, it seems to me that people are encouraged to be weak. Harmony is not conducive to progress, to intellectual growth, to competition and the masculine traits. Christianity instills in human beings a tendency to deny egocentric drives that animate every individual. Such Christian concepts have become ineffective in worldly affairs. They deny human beings individualism and give them no defense against their enemies. So, I would have to say that a harmonious ethics is, indeed, weak.

JM: I find it hard to believe that you equate harmony with weakness. In your philosophy you contend that a strong prince can bring harmony to a society.

NM: You are right there. But this harmony is achieved by the forceful elimination of friction. Power again, the essential smooth-running of the state. But generally society cannot be harmonious, certainly not for very long. It is best to recognize that and make sure that you are not among the exploited portion of society. It is much better to exploit than to be exploited. I think most people, in spite of their ethical protestations, sense that. But only a few of them are strong-willed enough to survive mediocrity. One must be a cunning and crafty *virtuoso*, as I have said, in order to keep out in front of the crowd, lazy and uninspired as it is.

JM: But doesn't conventional morality not only bring harmony in journalism--and between journalism and society--but also reinforce the concept of freedom?

NM: No, it is the *princely* journalist who follows my admonitions who is free from the pressure of custom and tradition. He also enjoys a very profound freedom, a freedom from allegiance to the conventional moral system of his society. He is free to use cruelty or piety toward his associates or audiences as circumstances dictate, adjusting quickly to every variation of fortune. He holds to the conventional good if he can, but enters into evil when he must.

JM: Would you say that what you have just said is a kind of *anti-ethics*, rather than a real ethics?

NM: Not really. It is a "real" ethics, whatever you might mean by that. It is what I have called *public* or pragmatic ethics. And I think most American journalists would be able to relate to my kind of ethics. They might not want to admit that they largely agree with it, but they really do. If they are leaders, if they are successful, if they have power and exercise it, if they manage people in their work, then they know the value of cunning and the need for virtuosity and courage in assuring their continuing success.

JM: Another question, Nick. I think I know how you feel about Kant's formalistic duty-ethics, but what about the ethical imperative of Jesus to the effect that we should act toward others as we would want them to act toward us? Is this not a basic, universal principle of morality?

NM: Well, let me say a few things about this "Golden Rule." First, it is really a self-centered maxim, not an altruistic one as it is often considered. Do something because you want something. Don't do it because it is simply *right*. Consider the consequences--to *yourself*--before you act. That seems to be what Jesus is saying. And, of course, Confucius said it in negative form long before Jesus' time. So, really, Jesus and I don't differ too much much in this respect.

JM: Do you mean that it is not a worthy ethical principle, then?

NM: No. That's not what I mean. I think it *is* a good ethical principle-- although I wonder if Kant would think so. You recall that *he* would have us act *only* from a sense of duty, not from any personal or selfish motivation with an expectation of good consequences. The Golden Rule is indeed a good ethical principle for most people--but not such a good one for those who want power and success. The journalist, for example, would commit reportorial suicide if he followed such a principle. As a journalist I might not want to have my action publicized if I were caught in a criminal activity; therefore, as a journalist I would not write the story about the criminal activity of another. What would become of journalism if all journalists followed the Golden Rule?

JM: Following up on that last question, Nick, how do you feel about the importance of religion in the development of a journalism ethics? We are often told by demographic surveyors that American journalists are in the main not religious. If so, how would it affect their ethics?

NM: I mentioned religion earlier today, but will add to what I said. I really am of two minds on that question you just asked. First, I have long had the sense that the best means of developing good habits among people is found in religion, and that the founders of religions probably deserve more praise than the founders of nations.

JM: Why?

NM: Because unless the people fear God, they will not follow state laws they feel incomprehensible. In a way, religion rallies divine authority to support political goals, helping unite the people and making the task of leaders easier. In journalism, I think religious dedication would help keep journalists calm and willing to be led and to do dull tasks.

JM: You said you were of *two minds* on this question. What is the other way you look at it?

NM: I have some misgivings about a religion such as Christianity that tends to separate people from the real world. It makes them contemplative and other-worldly, and causes them to have little use for practical affairs of the world. This can do great harm to them, and it makes them difficult to lead. For the sake of authenticity and individualism it is probably a good thing your journalists are not very religious.

JM: What do you mean by that last statement?

NM: Well, non-religious persons are more authentic than religious persons. They are more involved in the business of the state; they are more vigorous, more innovative, and have much stronger wills. They understand worldly honor and have a greater desire to excel, to distinguish themselves through noble acts, and worldly accomplishments. And they tend not to be so "soft" in their relations with others that they put themselves in danger. Remember what happened when my friend, Savonarola, who was an humble man, turned the other cheek, and tried to set up a religious republic in Florence?

JM: What happened to him?

NM: Well, in 1498 his experiment ended in excommunication and death by being burned at the stake. I prefer the virile Roman ethic of the safety of the people, with the state being the supreme law.

JM: But, relating this to journalism, why would not a Christian journalist be able to be vigorous and innovative, traits that you admire?

NM: The Christian journalist would focus much his attention on the transcendent "beyond," turning himself and others from worldly affairs and thereby discouraging the development of *virtù*. Also he would glorify the humble and the meditative instead of the bold and heroic. This concern with spiritual matters is the primary cause of his weakness and his inability to strive for success. The Church is but a projection of the individual, and as such, it must serve the state, not the other way around. A good example of what happens when religion gets the upper hand is the Holy Roman Empire, which had a very hard fall.

JM: Now, how does this apply to ethics?

NM: Only in a tangential way, I suppose. It might mean, of course, that only the person tied to his own *virtù*, and not to various mythologies of religion is the truly free--and therefore, ethical--person. Much of what is done in journalism or in other aspects of life, of course results from the actions of *Fortuna* and not from a person's will, but at least fifty percent of our actions are self-determined.

JM: Would you say a little more about *Fortuna*?

NM: I've written much about that, but I'll give you a brief idea here. *Fortuna*, or fate as you might call her, does not necessarily bestow benefits only, as is often thought. Unlike Providence, intending good for humanity, *Fortuna* may even seek its ruin. But, and this is important, we still have freedom to a considerable degree. *Fortuna,* as I just said, rules only half our actions, leaving us to determine the other half.. Even with a person like me, one who puts great faith in the power of *virtù*, *Fortuna* has shown me very little consideration for the good. She has kept me from succeeding as I wanted in government service. She has had me thrown in prison and tortured. And she has virtually exiled me here to my little farm. But, I suppose that, through being a rather adept *virtuoso*, I have overcome much of her impact and have made some worthy contributions.

JM: I think *Fortuna* has not treated you too badly, Nick. But what would you say to the journalist who must contend daily with the ups and downs of *Fortuna*? Do you think that the bold journalist can have considerable power over your *Fortuna*?

NM;   Yes, I do. I think of Fortune as a woman, easily mastered by the forceful and the bold. Only when she is not resisted, she evidences her great power. She usually retreats when confronted by the leader with *virtù*. It is only when the person is using *virtù*, and not succumbing to the passive enticements of *Fortuna*, that he manifests his humanity and individual potency. And I consider this essential for any kind of ethics.

JM: But, Nick, you yourself have been maltreated by *Fortuna*. How is it that your *virtù* did not serve you better in this contest?

NM: I am a strong advocate of the use of *virtù*, but this does not mean that I am myself as dedicated to it as I should be. Many times I have been weak and passive, giving in to the seduction of powerful others, falling for the enticements of Christian morality. Thus I have made myself vulnerable to the dictates of Dame Fortune.

JM: Well, Nick, I'm sorry that we must close this session. With what you have said earlier and what you have said today, I think I understand your general view of ethics. You have given me a good overview of your very interesting philosophy in this series of interviews, and I thank you very much. I do appreciate your taking time these last two weeks to talk with me. It has been most enlightening. I wish you all the best with your future endeavors. I must be on my way now. Farewell.

Chapter 15

Postscript to the Interviews

The dozen interviews recorded above, I think, provide many interesting insights into Machiavelli's ideas about journalism. He was the consummate pragmatist in his comments on the press, as might have been expected, but I found him occasionally to be somewhat naive about American journalism. For one thing, he tended to ascribe selfish motives to *everything* the journalist does. Perhaps he was thinking too much about the harsh realities of politics in the 15th and 16th centuries. We know today that journalists, far more than politicians, tend to have an idealistic, altruistic streak At least a large number of them do. And this tempers their striving for personal power and selfish ends; in other words, it tempers their *machiavellianism.*

Although I disagreed with almost all of what Machiavelli said in the interview sessions, I tried to restrain my argumentative nature and to hide my general distaste for what he was saying. I think I succeeded, although perhaps by so doing, I was being less than authentic and was using a somewhat Machiavellian tactic myself to keep him talking with me.

Machiavelli certainly placed power and self-agrandizement in the center of his philosophy of journalism. But he was no fool. He realized, as he intimated several times in the interviews, that other people--because of the social realities--are vitally important in a pragmatic sense. In other words, he seemed convinced that one *must* think of the public in order to succeed in producing profitable journalism.

The interviews, in most respects, went smoothly. Machiavelli listened attentively to my questions. His answers were precise, sometimes tinged with a slight note of humor--and occasionally with a spark of cynicism and bitterness.

From to time to time he would wander away from the question, during which wanderings I would listen patiently, but I would take no notes. He especially liked to discourse on Biblical characters--Old Testament ones who were strong and determined--and Roman stalwarts like Livy and Seneca. In spite of the fact that he had insisted that we keep the interviews short, he was prone to lapses of non-journalistic asides, from which I had to rescue him from time to time.

During his extra-interview musings, he would get into areas of personal interest, from which I would, after letting him have considerable leeway, bring him back to our journalistic topic. He enjoyed thinking out loud about his image in the world, and would often rather sadly lament the world's demeaning of him and his ideas. He reminded me more than once that, although he had not fared well in history, his words cannot be ignored because people intuitively know that they clearly describe the world as it really is.

By the end of the interviews, although I did not agree with his basic journalistic philosophy, I had a certain sympathy for him. He was probably more guilty of excess than of immorality; he certainly would have failed the test of Aristotle's Golden Mean, veering strongly toward personal pragmatics and away from altruistic utilitarianism. And, if he were immoral, it may well be that it was due to his teachings, and not in his own *private* or personal thought and action. This, however, is problematic, and even after a month of interviews with him, I certainly was not sure just who the real Machiavelli was. It seemed to me that he was simply dazzled by his own virtuosity, cleverness, and skill at deceiving and manipulating people. I feel that he was often deceiving me and that he was indeed a great dissembler. I am not sure that I escaped his virtuosity.

Machiavelli was a good speaker, usually keeping his talks with me on a rather informal level. He especially enjoyed reminiscing about his early government service, beginning in 1498 when the renowned Friar Girolamo Savonarola's regime fell from power in Florence. It was then that Machiavelli first held office, as a new government was formed in the wake of the change. He talked of how much he enjoyed his job as secretary to the main foreign relations committee of the new Florentine republic. It was during the next fourteen years, he said, that he did his most interesting work--going on a number of diplomatic missions throughout Europe and writing a large number of official reports. It was during this time, he recalled, that he learned to appreciate the tremendous problems faced by any reporter in attempting to write "objectively."

About the only interruption in the interview sessions was a brief tea-time (brandy-time, really) in which Machiavelli sipped slowly as he made comments on one or more of his children, his wife Marietta Corsini, his attendance at literary gatherings at the Oricellari Gardens in Florence, and that "strange man, Savonarola," on his fellow (though younger) historiographer Guiccardini, on his good friend Francesco Vettori (with whom he corresponded often), and on the flock of geese that seemed always to surround the house. At one or more sessions, during the break, he had dropped the names of such contemporary notables as Lorenzo di Medici, Cesare Borgia, and Cardinal Giulio di Medici (later Pope Clement VII) from whom he had just received a commission to write the history of Florence.

Machiavelli seemed always happy to take such a recess or break from the actual interviews. It was at these times that he said some very interesting things. More than once he reprimanded me gently about calling him "Nick," saying that it seemed rather informal, or even "cute," in the more staid Florentine environment. I told him that my wife, Dorothy, had said the same thing, even using the word "cute." He noted the insightful nature of women, but warned that they must be kept in check or they would take over the world.

On another occasion, he commented on my manner of dress, noting that my blue coat was rather loud as was my red tie. He noted that in Florence most everyone wore black or brown. "When in Florence," he said, "you should do as the Florentines do." I told him that I thought that was said about Rome. "The Romans want to take credit for everything," he said, "but actually it was said here first, and it was said about Florence not Rome."

At one session Machiavelli referred to Rome again, saying that it was really a city-state that produced very little. "Its main contributions have been made by people of the Italian peninsula who have gone to Rome to do their work." His belief was that Rome was not as energetic and creative as Florence, or Milan, or Venice. Or even Genoa, he added. Genoa claims Columbus, a good harbor, and good leather goods, Machiavelli observed. "Actually Columbus is over in your New World right now, I think, trying to make the Indians into Christians and to relieve them of their gold and silver."

Machiavelli continued, "I don't think Columbus was really from Genoa. My investigations have led me to believe that he was a Catalán, and that he came from somewhere northwest of Barcelona near the monastery of Monserrat."

I told him that his last comment was quite surprising, that my son Charles had been researching Columbus for years and believed, too, that he was from Catalunia, from the general area north of Monserrat near the town of Cervera. "After all," I said, "Columbus never referred to himself or signed letters using the name *Colombo* (Italian); instead he always used the name

Colum (Catalán) or *Colón (Spanish)."*

Often it was difficult to get Machiavelli back into the interviews about journalism. He was anxious to talk about a large number of subjects. But he would get back to the subject under discussion when I insisted. During the interview periods Machiavelli paid little attention to my rather awkward scribbling and proceeded calmly answering my questions as if I were an accomplished court reporter. From time to time he would glance, with some obvious irritation, out the window behind him as two aggressive geese honked insistently at one another. One of the strangest things about the sessions with Machiavelli was that I never met any other person in the house, although I had reason to believe there were others there.

Often during the interviews, I felt that Machiavelli *knew* that I was wondering if anyone else were in the house and who that person might be. And I sensed that he was enjoying the fact that I was so mystified. From time to time, as he talked, he would glance quickly toward what I assumed was the door to the kitchen. And, accompanying the quick glance, the briefest smile appeared on his thin lips.

At the end of the final session, on the fifteenth of August, 1520, I gathered up my notes and edged toward the door. Offering no small talk on my departure, Machiavelli simply rose from his straight chair, offered his hand, and bade me farewell and success. I made my way through the small hallway, opened the heavy door, and let myself out into the warm, sultry Italian air.

* * *

Now that I am back in the United States and living at the changing years of the century and the millennium, and after reflecting on my fascinating interviews with Machiavelli in a time long gone, I think I should try to clarify a few points, especially as they relate to my own position in journalism.

As I re-read those questions and answers recorded during those sultry days of 1520, I am aware that some readers may think that I surreptitiously have sympathy with the views of Machiavelli. Certainly I gave him the opportunity to express his views as he wished, and admittedly I treated him and many of his expressions with courtesy, and did not really try to argue or debate with him. Nevertheless, I think the careful reader will note that, in the interviews, my own ideas about journalistic freedom and ethics were not consistent with those of Machiavelli.

Undoubtedly, Machiavelli and his ideas have an appeal for many modern American journalists. And some of his insights are engaging, even enticing. And some of them are undoubtedly valid: that is, consistent with modern psychological, sociological, and political thinking. For our society is, indeed, highly competitive and pragmatic, often consumed by frenzied pursuit of success. And if the lure of Machiavelli's ideas came across in the interviews, it is not because I fancy, endorse, or recommend them; rather it is the intrinsic and enduring predilection to them that seems to reside in all people of ambition and spirit. Such a predilection, from a Judeo-Christian moral perspective at least, must not be pampered and utilized; it must be constantly challenged and expurgated by the journalist of integrity and authenticity, difficult as that often is.

Let me make my position very clear: *Machiavellianism in journalism is anathema to me*, and I conducted these interviews not as an endorsement, but as a warning, to give an airing to what I think is a growing struggle for power in modern American journalism.

I, like many observers of the modern press, am constantly startled, even appalled, by the many instances of arrogant journalistic power. Shocking cases of media abuse, such as the persistent and fatal harrassment of Princess Diana in 1997, have elicited flurries of apologies and vitriolic denials from a harried press intent on protecting its freedom and power. Machiavelli continues to make his mark on modern journalism.

As today's journalists become ever more enthralled by what they call "investigative reporting," where *success* is the nourishment of power, the lure of Machiavelli's teachings is increasingly potent. And it is indeed strange that, as talk and study of ethics become more prevalent among journalists, in practice the pragmatic "non-ethics" (or "public ethics") of Machiavelli has not loosened its grip.

This is a sad situation, made even sadder by the inauthentic protestations of moral concern rising from journalists and journalism students. It may well be true, as many say, that beneath the patina of Judeo-Christian ethics governing most American jourenalists lies a deep-seated Machiavellian drive. But if it *is* true, American journalists would do well to root it out and act from humane principles rather than expediency and self-aggrandizement.

In spite of all his charm, wit, and sophistic argument, Niccolò Machiavelli (his teachings, at least) is indeed devilish and destructive to conventional morality. The American journalist who *really* wants to be ethical will recognize the Florentine thinker for what he really was {a spokesman for the dark side of humanity} and will forsake his so-called *public* (or "non-ethics") as personally demeaning and socially destructive.

Appendix A

Ten Commandments for Journalists

(Suggested to the author by Machiavelli during the interviews in San Casciano, near Florence, in 1520)

1. *Have no Gods but the God of Success.*

Achieving your ends is the untimate journalistic purpose. You must use power whenever possible to gain your ends, for weakness is the prelude to ineffective and sterile journalism.

2. *Create, however, false Gods in order to make the people think they are sharing in your power.*

For example, create Codes of Ethics and Press Councils, make people think you are community-spirited and are bringing them into your daily journalistic decisions. Also repeat often mystical phrases such as "the people's right to know" and "dedication to the truth."

3. *Always advocate Truth--your truth, stemming from your Power and your Purpose.*

Be sure that the people always get their "right to know" even if it is a mythical right--but make certain that you decide what they have a right to know; you determine the truth that they will know. Never forget it.

4. *Never tamper with the Truth unless such tampering will enhance your Authority and Power, accomplish your purpose, and assure public conformity and stability.*

The God of Truth is a false God, to be used only to lure the unsuspecting person to a sense of knowledge that is convenient to your purposes. Always bow to this God in public, but always have a hidden smile on your face.

5. *Recognize that Justice is the handmaiden of Truth in the minds of the people. Therefore proclaim both constantly.*

Truth is a cold concept and often frightens the people, while Justice is a warm concept that must be used to temper the rigor of Truth and make the people feel that the Press is truly virtuous. Make the people think you are being both truthful and just although you know that this is usually impossible. Remember: you can fool most of the people most of the time.

6. *Recognize that the people prize Power even more than the concepts of Truth and Justice, and act accordingly.*

Get power, keep power, use power, and enlarge power. Never foolishly relinquish it for altruism's sake. Remember that you have the first and last word in public discourse. You set the agenda. The people expect very little of substance from you. Make sure you do not disappoint them.

7. *Recognize that Journalism is really beyond Ethics and that you are not accountable to anybody or anything except perhaps Market Forces and your own conscience.*

Always trust your self-interested conscience, and as for the Market, remember that when the existing Press is the only game in town, it will not be forsaken by the people.

8. *Never commit plagiarism--except where adequate camouflaging is possible.*

Use only those things of others that are helpful to your own cause; eschew in your plagiarizing any poorly written or ineffective material--and certainly never steal any material that might harm your position or cause.

9. *Obey laws and conventional morality except when they interfere with your objective.*

Generally it is good to obey laws; it is much like telling a half-truth. And don't forget: since Truth and the People's Right to Know are prized in the mythology of the masses, use any means possible to extol the impossible Truth and fulfill the non-existent Right to Know. At least tell the people that you pay allegiance to such objectives. They will usually believe you.

10. *Never admit a moral or legal transgression.*

Always fall back on the First Amendment and traditional journalistic freedom to justify any action you feel is consistent with your Purpose. Never let the people forget that freedom is far more important than somebody's sense of responsibility. And remember that ethics is *your ethics*, not theirs.

Appendix B

Highlights of Machiavelli's Life

1469   May 3, born in Florence, the son of a jurist.

1494   The Medici expelled from Florence. Machiavelli appointed clerk in the Second Chancery of the new republic.

1498   Machiavelli becomes Second Chancellor and Secretary of the Florentine Republic. In May the puritanical Dominican friar Girolamo Savonarola, who was the main influence in Florence's government, went to the gallows and was burned.

1500   Machiavelli sent to France; meets Louis XII and the Cardinal of Rouen.

1502   Marries Marietta Corsini. Posted to Romagna (an area in northeastern Italy) as envoy to Cesare Borgia who had a great influence on his political philosophy. Witnessed events leading to Borgia's murder.

1503   Returns to Florence in January.

1504   Second mission to France.

1506   In December he submits a plan to reorganize the military to Pierre Soderini, the gonfalonier of Florence, and it was accepted.

1508   Sent to Bolzano to the court of Holy Roman Emperor Maximilian I.

1510   Third and final mission to France.

1512   The Medici return with a Spanish army. Machiavelli mobilized a small army of 12,000 to repel the invasion, but his poorly-equipped citizen army was unable to withstand the seasoned Spanish forces. Florence deposes Soderini and welcomes the Medici.

1513   Machiavelli implicated in a conspiracy against the Medici. Thrown into prison; maintained his innocence even under torture. Released from prison, but restrictions put on his freedom. Reduced to poverty, he sought refuge in his little property inherited from his father at San Casiano. Completed his two most famous books *The Prince* and *The Discourses*

1519   Consulted by the Medici on a new constitution for Florence.

1520   Commissioned to write a history of Florence. Published *The Art of War* and *The Life of Castruccio Castracane*. (**Interviewed at San Casciano on the subject of American journalism**)

1526   Pope Clement VII employs Machiavelli to inspect the fortifications of Florence and to consult with this historian Francesco Guicciardini.

1527   June 21, dies. Buried in the small churchyard at Santa Croce, where other great Florentine figures such as Michelangelo and Galileo, also rest. (Citizens of Florence, in the 18th century, erected a monument to his memory, simply incribed: "No praise can enhance such a great name.")

Select Bibliography

Bock, Gisela, Quentin Skinner, and Maurizio Viroli. *Machiavelli and Republicanism*. Cambridge: Cambridge University Press, 1990.

Coyle, Martin (ed.). *Niccolo Machiavelli's The Prince: New Interdisciplinary Essays*. Manchester: Manchester University Press, 1995.

De Grazia, Sebastian. *Machiavelli in Hell*. Princeton: Princeton University Press, 1989.

Garver, Eugene. *Machiavelli and the History of Prudence*. Madison: University of Wisconsin Press, 1987.

Hulling, Mark. *Citizen Machiavelli*. Princeton: Princeton University Press, 1983.

Kahn, Victoria. *Machiavellian Rhetoric*. Princeton: Princeton University Press, 1994.

Machiavelli, N. *The Discourses* (many editions).

———————. *The Prince (*many editions).

Mansfield, Harvey C., Jr. (trans.). *The Prince*. Chicago: University of Chicago Press, 1985.

Najemy, John M. *Between Friends: Discourses of Power and the Desire in the Machiavelli-Vettori Letters of 1513-1515*. Princeton: Princeton University Press, 1993.

Nietzsche, Friedrich. *Beyond Good and Evil* (trans. & commentary by Walter Kaufmann). New York: Vintage Books (Random House), 1966.

Nell, Onora. *Acting on Principle: An Essay on Kantian Ethics.* New York: Columbia University Press, 1975.

Parel, Anthony J. *The Machiavellian Cosmos.* New Haven: Yale University Press, 1992.

Rebhorn, Wayne A. *Foxes and Lions: Machiavelli's Confidence Men.* Ithaca: Cornell University Press, 1988.

Skinner, Quentin. *Machiavelli.* New York: Hill and Wang, 1981.

Tarlton, Charles D. *Fortune's Circle: A Biographical Interpretation of Niccolò Machiavelli.* Chicago: Quadrangle Books, 1970.

Van Paassen, Pierre. *A Crown of Fire: The Life and Times of Girolomo Savonarola.* New York: Charles Scribner's Sons, 1960.

Villari, Pasquale. *The Life and Times of Niccolò Machiavelli* (trans. by Linda Vallari). London: Ernest Benn Ltd., 1891. Republished by Scholarly Press, St. Clair Shores, Mich., 1929.

Index

Acton, Lord, 26
advertising, 19, 98
agenda-setting, 20, 30
Alice (in Wonderland), 56
Altruism, 53
American journalistic tradition, 2
Aristotle, 122
Arte della Guerra (Machiavelli), 5
audience, respect for, 18

Bangladesh, 1
Barcelona, 123
Barron, Jerome, 80
Berlin, Isaiah, xiv, 47, 113
Bolzano, 132
Borgia, Cesare, 5, 11 123, 131

Castro, Fidel, 70
Catalán, 123-24
Catalunia, 123
Categorical Imperative, 103
Cave (Plato), 17, 93
Censorship, 68
Cervera, 123
China, 1
Christian morality, ix, 103, 114-16
Christianity, Machiavelli on, 19
Church, 92, 96-7, 117

civic journalism, 81-83
Clement VII (Pope), 123. 130
"collective will," 27
Columbus, 123-24
communitarians, 2, 12, 66
Confucius, 116
Congress, U.S., 71
conventional ethics (see private ethics), 111-12
Corsini, Marietta (NM's wife), 123, 131
Counter-Reformation (of Church), 5
credibility of the press, 38
Croce, Benedetto, xiv
crowd psychology, 96

Dame Fortune (see *fortuna*), 93, 119
Dewey, John, 28
DiMedici, Giulio (Pope Clement VII), 123
DiMedici, Lorenzo, 35, 123
Discourses (Machiavelli), 3, 6, 10
diversity of the press, 69

editorial autonomy, 2
education, Machiavelli on, 13-15
egalitarianism, 112

egocentric institution, journalism
    as, 29-30
Ellul, Jacques, 96
Enlightenment (Europe), 2, 18,
    82
Europe, 4
executive branch (of
    government), 71

fairness in journalism, 67-68
Fallows, James, 84
Far East, 60
First Amendment (to U.S.
    Constitution), 24, 29, 36, 71
Florence, xvi, 1, 4, 5, 8, 10, 15,
    95, 117, 122-23, 131
Fortuna, 118-19
Founding Fathers (of USA), 71
Fourth Branch of Government, 36
France, 4
freedom, 25; as anarchy, 44; from
    the press, 92; in government,
    92

Galileo, 132
game, journalism as, 21-22
Genoa, 123
God, 117
Golden Mean (Aristotle), 123
Golden Rule (Jesus), 116
Greece, 12
Guiccardini, 123, 132

historian, as reporter, 87-88
Hobbes, Thomas, 2, 3, 67
Hoffer, Eric, 75, 77
Holy Roman Empire, 118,132
Hutchins Commission, 3
Hutchins, Robert, 28

image, 19, 20, 26
Internet, 72
inauthenticity, Machiavelli on, 19

Jefferson, Thomas, 2, 70, 72
Jesus, 116
journalism, power of, 2, 7; good,
    20, 23
Judeo-Christian morality, 17-18
Justinus, 6

Kant, Immanuel, ix, 22, 53, 68,
    89, 103, 116
Kantian morality, 4, 68, 116
Korzybski, Alfred, 89

*La Vita di Castruccio
    Gastracanida Lucca* (NM
    book), 6
leadership, 20
Leviathan (Hobbes), 2
liberalism, Enlightenment, 2
"license" in journalism, 49
Lincoln, Abraham, 77
Lippmann, Walter, 3, 11, 75
Livy, 6, 122
Locke, John, 2, 18
Lorenzo di Medici, 123
lying, justification of, 105

Machiavelli, as ethicist, 4; as
    deontologist, 4; as enthroning
    "ends," 4; as pragmatist, 5;
    interview style, 6-7, on deceit
    in journalism, 11, on classical
    education; on good
    journalism, 20, 23, on power,
    4; on success, 4, 25-26; on
    rhetorical mannerisms, 6, 83;
    appearance, 6-7; on

technology, 7; on being feared, 12; on education, 13-14; on self-respect, 18; on soldiers and journalists, 61-62; on women, 20-21, 121
Madison, James, 2
Mao Zedung, 69
Mark Twain, on egoism, 55
masses, as impotent, 19
Maximilian I, 132
Meineche, Friedrich, xiv
Merrill, Charles (JM's son), 123
Merrill, Dorothy (JM's wife), 123
Michelangelo, 132
Mill, John Stuart, 2, 18, 28, 45, 111-12
Monserrat, 123

natural right, 18
negative freedom, 47
news, lack of definition, 39
Nietzsche, 45, 60-61, 68
Nigeria, 1

objectivity (journalistic), as a myth, 87-88
"Old Nick," 3, 7, 9
Old Testament, 122
opiate for the people, journalism as, 30
Oricellari Gardens (Florence), 123
Overman (Superman) of Nietzsche, 45

Parel, Anthony, xiv
"people's press," 80
"perceptive strainers," Machiavelli on, 87

philosophers (Marxist), 66
philosophy, journalism's lack of, 39
Plato, 12, 44, 77, 93
political correctness, 20
Pope Clement, 10, 95, 123, 132
positive freedom, 47
power, in journalism, 23-24
power machine, journalism as, 26
pragmatic egoist, 110
pragmatic ethics, 112
pragmatics, 112
pragmatism, 67
predetermined ends, 37
press, as *leviathan*, 2; as princely, 23
press control, freedom from, 90
Prince, The (Machiavelli), 1, 3, 5, 11, 19, 20, 25, 74, 101, 104, 110
private ethics (see conventional ethics), 20, 52, 63, 105
propaganda, as rhetoric, 97
Providence, 118
pseudo-world, as created by press, 91-92
psychiatrists, 80
public, as fickle, 44
public ethics, 63, 113, 125
public (see civic) journalism, 2, 19-20, 74
public opinion, 75
public relations, 19, 53, 78

Rand, Ayn, 62
Rawls, John, 28
religion, effect on ethics, 114-15
Renaissance, x, 2,
Republic, The (Plato), 12, 43
responsibility, moral view, 54

rhetoric, Machiavelli on, 83
"right of access" (by public) to
    press, 80
"right to know" (public), 28-29,
80-81
Romagna, 129
Rome, 6, 15, 43, 93, 121
Ronciglione, Raulo da, 14

San Casciano, 4, 5, 130
Santa Croce, 130
Savonarola, 115, 120, 129
Schopenhauer, 60-61
    semantics, 46

Seneca, 120
Sherrill, Bob, x, 51-52
Smith, Adam, 3
social control, mission of
    journalism, 26
Society of Professional
    Journalists, 90
Socrates, 12, 43, 77
Soderini, Pierre, 129, 130
soldiers, compared to journalists,
    61-62
sophists, 43
Stalin, 69

state, as superior to state, 68
Strauss, Leo, xiv
success, essential for journalists,
    25-26
Supreme Court, 71

Tacitus, 6
teleological ethics, 109
Third World, 1, 92
Thrasymachus, 43-44
Tornillo case, 80
Tuscany, 121

University of Florence, 15, 35

"value pluralism" (Berlin), 113
Virgil, 6
virtù, 3, 13, 20, 107, 118-119
virtuoso, 12, 107, 112-13
Vettori, Francesco, 123
Voltaire, 2

will, as seen by Schopenhauer
    and Nietzsche, 60-61
Will, George, 11
women, in journalism, 20-21
world, as press-created, 92-93
World Wide Web, 72

About the Author

John C. Merrill has been a journalist, a university professor, and a foreign lecturer for nearly a half century. He retired officially in 1992 but has been teaching part-time as Professor Emeritus of Journalism at the University of Missouri-Columbia.

A native Mississippian, he holds four degrees: a B.A. in English and history from Mississippi Delta State University, an M.A. in journalism from Louisiana State University, a Ph.D. in mass communication from the University of Iowa, and an M.A. in philosophy from the University of Missouri.

He is the author or editor of some 25 books, among them *The Elite Press* (1968), *The Imperative of Freedom* (1974), *Existential Journalism* (1977, 1996), *The Dialectic in Journalism* (1990), *Legacy of Wisdom: Great Thinkers and Journalism* (1996), and *Journalism Ethics* (1997).

Dr. Merrill has lectured and held seminars and workshops for journalists in more than 50 countries--since 1990 in Russia, Egypt, Morocco, Pakistan, Spain, Germany, South Korea, Taiwan, and Israel and the West Bank.

He has been a Distinguished Visiting Professor at several universities-- National Chengchi University in Taiwan, the American University in Cairo, Birzeit University on the West Bank, the University of Virginia, California State University at Long Beach, and the University of Miami (Florida).

In 1987 he was a senior fellow at the Gannett Center for Media Studies (now Freedom Forum Media Studies Center) at Columbia University in New York City. He was won a number of journalism awards, the latest being the Honor Medal (1996) for distinguished service to journalism, given annually by the School of Journalism, University of Missouri.